OPPOSING VIEWPOINTS® SERIES

Artificial Intelligence

Other Books of Related Interest

Opposing Viewpoints Series
Digital Rights and Privacy
Personhood
Teens and Social Media

At Issue Series
Nuclear Anxiety
Populism in the Digital Age
The Role of Science in Public Policy

Current Controversies Series
Artificial Intelligence and the Future of Humanity
Big Tech and Democracy
Cyberterrorism

> "Congress shall make no law ... abridging the freedom of speech, or of the press."
>
> *First Amendment to the U.S. Constitution*

The basic foundation of our democracy is the First Amendment guarantee of freedom of expression. The Opposing Viewpoints series is dedicated to the concept of this basic freedom and the idea that it is more important to practice it than to enshrine it.

OPPOSING VIEWPOINTS® SERIES

Artificial Intelligence

Avery Elizabeth Hurt, Book Editor

GREENHAVEN PUBLISHING

Published in 2024 by Greenhaven Publishing, LLC
2544 Clinton Street,
Buffalo NY 14224

Copyright © 2024 by Greenhaven Publishing, LLC

First Edition

All rights reserved. No part of this book may be reproduced in any form without permission in writing from the publisher, except by a reviewer.

Articles in Greenhaven Publishing anthologies are often edited for length to meet page requirements. In addition, original titles of these works are changed to clearly present the main thesis and to explicitly indicate the author's opinion. Every effort is made to ensure that Greenhaven Publishing accurately reflects the original intent of the authors. Every effort has been made to trace the owners of the copyrighted material.

Cover image: Phonlamai Photo/Shutterstock.com

Library of Congress CataloginginPublication Data

Names: Hurt, Avery Elizabeth, editor.
Title: Artificial intelligence / edited by Avery Elizabeth Hurt.
Description: First edition. | New York : Greenhaven Publishing,
2024. | Series: Opposing viewpoints | Includes index.
Identifiers: ISBN 9781534509511 (pbk.) | ISBN 9781534509528 (library bound)
Subjects: LCSH: Artificial intelligence--Juvenile literature. | Artificial intelligence--Social aspects--Juvenile literature. | Electronic data processing--Juvenile literature.
Classification: LCC Q335.4 A784 2024 | DDC 006.3--dc23

Manufactured in the United States of America

Website: http://greenhavenpublishing.com

Contents

The Importance of Opposing Viewpoints   11
Introduction   14

Chapter 1: Does AI Pose an Existential Risk for Humanity?

Chapter Preface   18

1. Artificial Intelligence Could Lead to Extinction of Humanity   19
   Chris Vallance
2. AI Can Help Solve Environmental Challenges That Threaten Life on Earth   23
   United Nations Environment Programme (UNEP)
3. Tech Is Just a Tool   29
   Emily A. Vogels, Lee Rainie, and Janna Anderson
4. Artificial Intelligence Has the Potential to Revolutionize Health Care   37
   Angela Spatharou, Solveigh Hieronimus, and Jonathan Jenkins
5. An AI Pioneer Warns of the Dangers of AI Development   44
   Zoe Kleinman and Chris Vallance
6. Can AI Be Trusted?   49
   Mark Bailey

Periodical and Internet Sources Bibliography   53

Chapter 2: Is AI Conscious, or Will It Soon Become Conscious?

Chapter Preface   56

1. ChatGPT Can't Think   57
   Philip Goff
2. Will Artificial Intelligence Become Conscious?   62
   Subhash Kak

3. AI Sentience Is Still the Stuff of Sci-Fi   67
   Nir Eisikovits
4. Give AI Empathy and Ethics and It Will Benefit, Not Endanger, Humans   73
   Arshin Adib-Moghaddam
5. AI Will Never Be Truly Conscious   77
   Subhash Kak
6. The Concept of Consciousness Is Important to Ethical Debates About AI   81
   Elisabeth Hildt

Periodical and Internet Sources Bibliography   89

Chapter 3: Should Governments Regulate or Temporarily Pause AI Research?

Chapter Preface   92

1. We Need to Pause AI Research   93
   Laurie Clarke
2. How Congress Can Regulate AI   99
   Anjana Susarla
3. AI Has the Potential to Quickly Change the Global Military Power Balance   104
   James Johnson
4. The Government Should Never Get Involved with AI Development   107
   Robin Mitchell
5. Regulating AI Will Be Difficult, but We Must Get It Right   114
   S. Shyam Sundar, Cason Schmit, and John Villasenor
6. AI Must Be Regulated for the Public Good   121
   Tim Juvshik

Periodical and Internet Sources Bibliography   126

Chapter 4: Can AI Become Less Biased?

Chapter Preface — **129**

1. AI Will Be Biased as Long as the Field Is Mostly White and Mostly Male — **130**
   John MacCormick

2. AI Is Not Just Racist and Sexist; It's Ageist Too. — **136**
   Charlene Chu, Kathleen Leslie, Rune Nyrup, and Shehroz Khan

3. Biased AI in the Legal System Could Change the Face of Justice — **141**
   Morgiane Noel

4. To Reduce Bias in AI, We Need to Understand How It Got That Way — **146**
   Tobias Baer and Vishnu Kamalnath

5. AI in Health Care Poses a Threat if Biases Are Left Unchecked — **152**
   Hammaad Adam, Aparna Balagopalan, Emily Alsentzer, Fotini Christia, and Marzyeh Ghassemi

Periodical and Internet Sources Bibliography — **159**

For Further Discussion — **161**
Organizations to Contact — **163**
Bibliography of Books — **167**
Index — **169**

The Importance of Opposing Viewpoints

Perhaps every generation experiences a period in time in which the populace seems especially polarized, starkly divided on the important issues of the day and gravitating toward the far ends of the political spectrum and away from a consensus-facilitating middle ground. The world that today's students are growing up in and that they will soon enter into as active and engaged citizens is deeply fragmented in just this way. Issues relating to terrorism, immigration, women's rights, minority rights, race relations, health care, taxation, wealth and poverty, the environment, policing, military intervention, the proper role of government—in some ways, perennial issues that are freshly and uniquely urgent and vital with each new generation—are currently roiling the world.

If we are to foster a knowledgeable, responsible, active, and engaged citizenry among today's youth, we must provide them with the intellectual, interpretive, and critical-thinking tools and experience necessary to make sense of the world around them and of the all-important debates and arguments that inform it. After all, the outcome of these debates will in large measure determine the future course, prospects, and outcomes of the world and its peoples, particularly its youth. If they are to become successful members of society and productive and informed citizens, students need to learn how to evaluate the strengths and weaknesses of someone else's arguments, how to sift fact from opinion and fallacy, and how to test the relative merits and validity of their own opinions against the known facts and the best possible available information. The landmark series Opposing Viewpoints has been providing students with just such critical-thinking skills and exposure to the debates surrounding society's most urgent contemporary issues for many years, and it continues to serve this essential role with undiminished commitment, care, and rigor.

The key to the series's success in achieving its goal of sharpening students' critical-thinking and analytic skills resides in its title—

Opposing Viewpoints. In every intriguing, compelling, and engaging volume of this series, readers are presented with the widest possible spectrum of distinct viewpoints, expert opinions, and informed argumentation and commentary, supplied by some of today's leading academics, thinkers, analysts, politicians, policy makers, economists, activists, change agents, and advocates. Every opinion and argument anthologized here is presented objectively and accorded respect. There is no editorializing in any introductory text or in the arrangement and order of the pieces. No piece is included as a "straw man," an easy ideological target for cheap point-scoring. As wide and inclusive a range of viewpoints as possible is offered, with no privileging of one particular political ideology or cultural perspective over another. It is left to each individual reader to evaluate the relative merits of each argument—as they see it, and with the use of ever-growing critical-thinking skills—and grapple with their own assumptions, beliefs, and perspectives to determine how convincing or successful any given argument is and how the reader's own stance on the issue may be modified or altered in response to it.

This process is facilitated and supported by volume, chapter, and selection introductions that provide readers with the essential context they need to begin engaging with the spotlighted issues, with the debates surrounding them, and with their own perhaps shifting or nascent opinions on them. In addition, guided reading and discussion questions encourage readers to determine the authors' point of view and purpose, interrogate and analyze the various arguments and their rhetoric and structure, evaluate the arguments' strengths and weaknesses, test their claims against available facts and evidence, judge the validity of the reasoning, and bring into clearer, sharper focus the reader's own beliefs and conclusions and how they may differ from or align with those in the collection or those of their classmates.

Research has shown that reading comprehension skills improve dramatically when students are provided with compelling, intriguing, and relevant "discussable" texts. The subject matter of these collections could not be more compelling, intriguing, or urgently relevant to today's students and the world they are poised to inherit. The anthologized articles and the reading and discussion questions that are included with them also provide the basis for stimulating, lively, and passionate classroom debates. Students who are compelled to anticipate objections to their own argument and identify the flaws in those of an opponent read more carefully, think more critically, and steep themselves in relevant context, facts, and information more thoroughly. In short, using discussable text of the kind provided by every single volume in the Opposing Viewpoints series encourages close reading, facilitates reading comprehension, fosters research, strengthens critical thinking, and greatly enlivens and energizes classroom discussion and participation. The entire learning process is deepened, extended, and strengthened.

For all of these reasons, Opposing Viewpoints continues to be exactly the right resource at exactly the right time—when we most need to provide readers with the critical-thinking tools and skills that will not only serve them well in school but also in their careers and their daily lives as decision-making family members, community members, and citizens. This series encourages respectful engagement with and analysis of opposing viewpoints and fosters a resulting increase in the strength and rigor of one's own opinions and stances. As such, it helps make readers "future ready," and that readiness will pay rich dividends for the readers themselves, for the citizenry, for our society, and for the world at large.

Introduction

> *"The benefits or harms are determined by how we humans choose to use tools and technologies. Fire can be used to cook a meal and thus be helpful. Fire can also be used to harm or destroy."*
>
> -David Bray, executive director for the People-Centered Internet Coalition

It's not often that the people who design a new product warn the public about the dangers it poses. But that's what happened with ChatGPT, a form of artificial intelligence (AI).

Before ChatGPT took the world by storm in 2022, most people thought of AI as something from science fiction, if they thought of it at all. Or maybe they knew that AI was being used to design new medicines or answer customer service requests (those chat bots that help you when you have an issue on a website). But most people didn't give AI much thought. ChatGPT was different, though. It was hard to ignore.

ChatGPT is a type of AI known as large language models (LLMs). LLMs are neural networks that are trained on ginormous amounts of text. (Neural networks are software designed to work in a way that resembles the way neurons in brains operate.)

As the name suggests, ChatGPT is designed to chat with humans about pretty much any topic. But that's not all it can do. It can write essays; it can help you plan a trip; it can even write computer code. It can make a lot of things faster and easier. Those customer service chat bots? They're much more helpful when powered by LLMs.

But this new AI also has a tendency to make things up. Computer experts call this hallucinating. That's a problem, but it's not the worst problem. ChatGPT and similar forms of AI can also be terribly racist and sexist. They quickly pick up from all the training data they're exposed to the worst things from our culture. They can spread misinformation and hate even faster than humans can. And unscrupulous humans can use this powerful new AI to cause plenty of trouble.

Because of all this—the good and the bad—the arrival of LLMs like ChatGPT has raised many complicated questions. The viewpoints in this book will explore four of those questions.

The authors in Chapter 1 tackle a very big question: Does AI pose an existential threat to humanity? As improbable as that scenario may seem, many people who know a lot about this new technology are taking it seriously. There are many ways AI could, with or without human help, take actions that could endanger humanity. How likely that is and what can be done about it are the themes of this chapter. Some authors think the threat is overblown. In fact, some argue that AI might even help *save* us.

Another question that seems a little strange at first is addressed in Chapter 2: Is AI conscious or might it soon become conscious? While most, though not all, experts agree that AI is not conscious (yet), the viewpoints in this chapter show how deeply experts are thinking about the possibility and what that would mean for humanity.

Given the concerns raised in the first two chapters, the authors in Chapter 3 deal with the question of whether governments should regulate or temporarily pause AI research. Considering the field of AI is evolving so quickly and certain innovations could have significant and unexpected implications, some advocates and politicians believe these potential outcomes deserve more consideration before the field is allowed to progress.

A more immediate concern about AI is the question of bias. AI as it exists today has an uncanny way of picking up on the worst in humans. It can be notoriously racist and biased in other ways too. Unfortunately, fixing that problem is more difficult than you might think. In Chapter 4, the authors discuss the difficulties of getting the bias out of AI and make suggestions for how to create less biased AI.

Humanity faces many complex and serious problems: climate change, nuclear weapons, loss of species diversity, increasing poverty, and inequality, among others. Now we can add dealing with advances in artificial intelligence to that list. Now that it's here, AI isn't going away. But perhaps the viewpoints shared in *Opposing Viewpoints: Artificial Intelligence* can help us think more deeply about how to best use this amazing technology in ways that help rather than harm us.

CHAPTER 1

Does AI Pose an Existential Risk for Humanity?

Chapter Preface

Recent advances in artificial intelligence technology have created a lot of excitement. The abilities of a type of AI known as large language models (LLMs)—the most well-known of these being ChatGPT—have convinced some people, including some AI experts, that they are already conscious. Most people doubt that AI is anywhere near being conscious. However, the abilities of these AI are uncanny. Even experts aren't sure what to make of them. For some, AI poses a potential existential threat, meaning a threat to our very existence. That may be a stretch. Or it may not.

This chapter features voices on both sides of the issue: Those who say AI poses a threat to humanity, and those who say that it might well be able to save us from ourselves. The chapter opens with a viewpoint about a very alarming letter from the people behind AI. The founders of the field of artificial intelligence as well as those who created the latest versions are sounding a warning about the dangers of AI.

However, other viewpoints in this chapter argue that AI is not so dangerous as that. In fact, they say the technology might be able to help solve a problem that *does* pose an existential threat to humanity: climate change. Yet another viewpoint looks at the potential for AI to revolutionize health care. According to these authors, AI can play an important role in addressing various societal issues.

Even the AI experts can't agree on the extent of the dangers posed by this astonishing new technology. But everyone does agree that it will change the world. The question is: How do we prepare for that?

VIEWPOINT 1

> "Mitigating the risk of extinction from AI should be a global priority alongside other societal-scale risks such as pandemics and nuclear war."

Artificial Intelligence Could Lead to Extinction of Humanity

Chris Vallance

In this viewpoint, journalist Chris Vallance, writing for the BBC, reports on an open letter warning of the dangers of AI. The letter was signed by hundreds of AI experts, including AI scientists and the heads of companies who created the technology. Some even argue that the existential threat posed by AI is comparable to that of nuclear weapons. But not everyone, Vallance finds, agrees that the threat is as serious as these experts fear. Chris Vallance is a technology reporter for the BBC.

As you read, consider the following questions:

1. Who are the people sounding the warning about the dangers of AI?
2. How, according to sources cited in this story, might AI further "fracture reality" and "erode the public trust?"
3. Some AI experts think the fear is overblown. What is their argument?

"Artificial intelligence could lead to extinction, experts warn," by Chris Vallance, BBC, May 30, 2023. Reprinted by permission.

Artificial Intelligence

Artificial intelligence could lead to the extinction of humanity, experts—including the heads of OpenAI and Google DeepMind—have warned.

Dozens have supported a statement published on the webpage of the Centre for AI Safety.

"Mitigating the risk of extinction from AI should be a global priority alongside other societal-scale risks such as pandemics and nuclear war" it reads.

But others say the fears are overblown.

Sam Altman, chief executive of ChatGPT-maker OpenAI; Demis Hassabis, chief executive of Google DeepMind; and Dario Amodei of Anthropic have all supported the statement.

The Centre for AI Safety website suggests a number of possible disaster scenarios:

- AIs could be weaponised—for example, drug-discovery tools could be used to build chemical weapons
- AI-generated misinformation could destabilise society and "undermine collective decision-making"
- The power of AI could become increasingly concentrated in fewer and fewer hands, enabling "regimes to enforce narrow values through pervasive surveillance and oppressive censorship"
- Enfeeblement, where humans become dependent on AI "similar to the scenario portrayed in the film *Wall-E*"

Dr. Geoffrey Hinton, who issued an earlier warning about risks from super-intelligent AI, has also supported the Centre for AI Safety's call.

Yoshua Bengio, professor of computer science at the university of Montreal, also signed.

Hinton, Bengio and NYU Professor Yann LeCun are often described as the "godfathers of AI" for their groundbreaking work in the field—for which they jointly won the 2018 Turing Award, which recognises outstanding contributions in computer science.

But LeCun, who also works at Meta, has said these apocalyptic warnings are overblown, tweeting that "the most common reaction by AI researchers to these prophecies of doom is face palming".

'Fracturing Reality'

Many other experts similarly believe that fears of AI wiping out humanity are unrealistic, and a distraction from issues such as bias in systems that are already a problem.

Arvind Narayanan, a computer scientist at Princeton University, has previously told the BBC that sci-fi-like disaster scenarios are unrealistic: "Current AI is nowhere near capable enough for these risks to materialise. As a result, it's distracted attention away from the near-term harms of AI".

Oxford's Institute for Ethics in AI senior research associate Elizabeth Renieris told BBC News she worried more about risks closer to the present.

"Advancements in AI will magnify the scale of automated decision-making that is biased, discriminatory, exclusionary, or otherwise unfair while also being inscrutable and incontestable," she said. They would "drive an exponential increase in the volume and spread of misinformation, thereby fracturing reality and eroding the public trust, and drive further inequality, particularly for those who remain on the wrong side of the digital divide".

Many AI tools essentially "free ride" on the "whole of human experience to date", Renieris said. Many are trained on human-created content, text, art, and music they can then imitate - and their creators "have effectively transferred tremendous wealth and power from the public sphere to a small handful of private entities".

But Centre for AI Safety director Dan Hendrycks told BBC News that future risks and present concerns "shouldn't be viewed antagonistically".

"Addressing some of the issues today can be useful for addressing many of the later risks tomorrow," he said.

Superintelligence Efforts

Media coverage of the supposed "existential" threat from AI has snowballed since March 2023 when experts, including Tesla boss Elon Musk, signed an open letter urging a halt to the development of the next generation of AI technology.

That letter asked if we should "develop non-human minds that might eventually outnumber, outsmart, obsolete and replace us."

In contrast, the new campaign has a very short statement, designed to "open up discussion."

The statement compares the risk to that posed by nuclear war. In a blog post OpenAI recently suggested superintelligence might be regulated in a similar way to nuclear energy: "We are likely to eventually need something like an IAEA [International Atomic Energy Agency] for superintelligence efforts" the firm wrote.

'Be Reassured'

Both Sam Altman and Google chief executive Sundar Pichai are among technology leaders to have discussed AI regulation recently with the prime minister.

Speaking to reporters about the latest warning over AI risk, Rishi Sunak stressed the benefits to the economy and society.

"You've seen that recently it was helping paralysed people to walk, discovering new antibiotics, but we need to make sure this is done in a way that is safe and secure," he said.

"Now that's why I met last week with CEOs of major AI companies to discuss what are the guardrails that we need to put in place, what's the type of regulation that should be put in place to keep us safe.

"People will be concerned by the reports that AI poses existential risks, like pandemics or nuclear wars.

"I want them to be reassured that the government is looking very carefully at this."

He had discussed the issue recently with other leaders, at the G7 summit of leading industrialised nations, Sunak said, and would raise it again in the United States soon.

VIEWPOINT 2

> "[AI] can help calculate the footprint of products across their full life cycles and supply chains and enable businesses and consumers to make the most informed and effective decisions."

AI Can Help Solve Environmental Challenges That Threaten Life on Earth

United Nations Environment Programme (UNEP)

In the previous viewpoint, many experts were concerned about the potential dangers of AI. This viewpoint from the United Nations Environment Programme (UNEP) considers some potential benefits of the technology. Because these benefits could help with environmental challenges, they could be as important to the survival of humanity as the risks discussed in the previous viewpoint were to humanity's extinction. The United Nations Environment Programme (UNEP) is the world's leading authority on the global environment.

As you read, consider the following questions:

1. According to this viewpoint, how might AI help deal with the climate crisis, biodiversity loss, and pollution?

"How artificial intelligence is helping tackle environmental challenges," United Nations Environment Programme (UNEP), November 7, 2022. Reprinted by permission.

2. What is the UNEP's World Environment Situation Room (WESR), and what is it doing to address environmental crises?
3. AI itself uses a lot of resources and can be a contributor to the problems this initiative is trying to solve. According to this viewpoint, how does the WESR plan to address that?

We can't manage what we don't measure, goes the old business adage. This rings true more than ever today as the world faces a triple planetary crisis of climate change, nature and biodiversity loss, pollution, and waste.

More climate data is available than ever before, but how that data is accessed, interpreted, and acted on is crucial to managing these crises. One technology that is central to this is artificial intelligence (AI).

So, what exactly does AI mean?

"AI refers to systems or machines that perform tasks that typically require human intelligence, and can iteratively improve themselves over time, based on the information they collect," says David Jensen, coordinator of the United Nations Environment Program's (UNEP's) Digital Transformation sub-program.

Jensen highlights several areas where AI can play a role in tackling environmental challenges, from designing more energy-efficient buildings to monitoring deforestation to optimizing renewable energy deployment.

"This can be on a large scale—such as satellite monitoring of global emissions, or a more granular scale—such as a smart house automatically turning off lights or heat after a certain time," he adds.

Informing Real-Time Analysis

UNEP's World Environment Situation Room (WESR), launched in 2022, is one digital platform that is leveraging AI's capabilities to analyze complex, multifaceted datasets.

Supported by a consortium of partners, WESR curates, aggregates, and visualizes the best available Earth observation and sensor data to inform near real-time analysis and future predictions on multiple factors, including CO_2 atmospheric concentration, changes in glacier mass, and sea level rise.

"WESR is being developed to become a user-friendly, demand-driven platform that leverages data into government offices, classrooms, mayors' offices, and boardrooms," says Jensen. "We need credible, trustworthy and independent data to inform decisions and drive transparency—WESR provides this," he adds.

"Over time, the goal is for WESR to become like a mission control center for planet Earth, where all of our vital environmental indicators can be seamlessly monitored to drive actions."

Monitoring Methane Emissions

One of the UNEP-led initiatives inside the WESR digital ecosystem is the International Methane Emissions Observatory (IMEO), which leverages AI to revolutionize the approach to monitoring and mitigating methane emissions.

The platform operates as a global public database of empirically verified methane emissions. It leverages AI to strategically interconnect this data with action on science, transparency, and policy to inform data-driven decisions.

"IMEO's technology allows us to collect and integrate diverse methane emissions data streams to establish a global public record of empirically verified methane emissions at an unprecedented level of accuracy and granularity," Jensen says.

"Reducing the energy sector's methane emissions is one of the quickest, most feasible, and cost-effective ways to limit the impacts of climate warming, and reliable data-driven action will play a big role in achieving these reductions," he adds.

Another environmental monitoring initiative that UNEP has cofounded, in partnership with IQAir, is the GEMS Air Pollution Monitoring platform. It is the largest global air quality information network in the world. IQAir aggregates data from over 25,000 air quality monitoring stations in more than 140 countries and leverages AI to offer insights on the impact of real-time air quality on populations and help inform health protection measures.

"These platforms allow both the private and public sector to harness data and digital technologies in order to accelerate global environmental action and fundamentally disrupt business as usual," Jensen says. "Ultimately, they can contribute to systemic change at an unprecedented speed and scale," he adds.

Measuring Environmental Footprints

Other areas where AI can make a difference is calculating the environmental and climate footprints of product. "AI will be fundamental in this area," Jensen says.

"It can help calculate the footprint of products across their full life cycles and supply chains and enable businesses and consumers to make the most informed and effective decisions. This kind of data is essential for sustainable digital nudging on e-commerce platforms such as Amazon.com. Shopify, or Alibaba."

FEARS OF EXISTENTIAL THREAT ARE OVERBLOWN

AI pioneer Yann LeCun has described talk of artificial intelligence (AI) posing an existential threat to humanity as "preposterously ridiculous."

Speaking to the BBC this week at an AI-focused event held in Paris by Meta, where he now works as the company's chief AI scientist, Professor LeCun said: "Will AI take over the world? No, this is a projection of human nature on machines."

LeCun's comments are in stark contrast to those made by Geoffrey Hinton and Yoshua Bengio, with whom he received the Turing Award in 2018 for breakthroughs in AI. The three experts are now often referred to as "the godfathers of AI."

Hinton recently quit his role at Google so he would be able to share his thoughts on AI development more freely. When asked in a recent CBS interview about the likelihood of AI "wiping out humanity," Hinton responded: "That's not inconceivable."

Bengio, meanwhile, said recently that while today's AI systems are nowhere near to posing an existential risk to humanity, it's possible that things could get "catastrophic" with more advanced versions of the technology, saying that there's "too much uncertainty" about where we might be with AI in a few years from now.

LeCun, however, appears more relaxed about the way things are going, saying that fears of AI taking over are overblown.

While the professor admitted that AI would undoubtedly surpass human intelligence, it would take years if not decades to reach that point. Even then, LeCun said, the idea that a superintelligent AI would escape our control is "just preposterously ridiculous," adding that it's simply "not the way anything works in the world."

LeCun told the BBC that even a highly advanced AI system is "going to run on a data center somewhere with an off switch. And if you realize it's not safe you just don't build it."

Viewing the technology in a more positive light, he said AI would lead to "a new renaissance for humanity" in a similar way to how the internet or the printing press transformed society.

While AI has been around for decades, recent and rapid advances in the technology have put it front and center, with powerful tools like OpenAI's ChatGPT and Google's Bard chatbots gaining much publicity for the impressive way in which they can handle data and converse in a human-like way.

"AI 'godfather' says fears of existential threat are overblown," by Trevor Mogg, Digital Trends Media Group, June 14, 2023.

Reducing ICT Emissions

While data and AI are necessary for enhanced environmental monitoring, there is an environmental cost to processing this data that we must also take into account, says Jensen.

"The ICT sector generates about 3 to 4 percent of emissions and data centers use large volumes of water for cooling. Efforts are underway to reduce this footprint—including through the CODES Action Plan for a Sustainable Planet in the Digital Age—one of the spin-off initiatives from the UN Secretary General's Roadmap for Digital Cooperation."

Artificial Intelligence

But e-waste is a major concern as only 17.4 percent is currently recycled and disposed of in an environmentally sound manner. According to the UN Global E-waste Monitor report, e-waste will grow to almost 75 million metric tons by 2030.

UNEP research shows that to target this waste, consumers should reduce consumption, recycle electronic goods, and repair those that can be fixed.

VIEWPOINT 3

> "The benefits or harms are determined by how we humans choose to use tools and technologies."

Tech Is Just a Tool

Emily A. Vogels, Lee Rainie, and Janna Anderson

The Pew Research Center, a nonpartisan center that informs citizens about issues shaping the world, surveyed a variety of experts to get their view on the dangers of AI. In this excerpted viewpoint, you'll read a few of those responses. Generally speaking, experts agree that AI can be used to benefit or harm humanity—it simply depends on how it is applied. Emily A. Vogels is a research associate focusing on the internet and technology at the Pew Research Center. Lee Rainie is the former director of internet and technology research at Pew; Janna Anderson, now a professor of journalism at Elon University, is a former senior contract researcher at Pew.

As you read, consider the following questions:

1. In this viewpoint, David Bray comments that "tech doesn't operate in a vacuum." What does he mean by that?
2. What form of resistance to the tech explosion is mentioned here? How is that happening?
3. What are some ways the experts in this viewpoint argue AI can be a tool for good?

"Tech is (just) a tool," by Emily A. Vogels, Lee Rainie, and Janna Anderson, Pew Research Center, June 30, 2020.

[…]

A pioneering technology editor and reporter for one of the world's foremost global news organizations wrote, "I don't believe technology will be the driver for good or bad in social and civil innovation. It can be a catalyst because it has always been a strong factor in organizing people and resources, as we saw early on with 'flash mobs' and have seen used to deleterious effect in the disinformation operations of Russian agents that sought to influence the 2016 U.S. presidential election. I believe the social and civic innovation that can rein in excesses of surveillance capitalism, of Big Brother tech such as the abuse of facial recognition and other biometrics for social control, can only come from moral leadership. Tech is a tool. Artificial intelligence and genetic engineering are technologies. How we choose to use these tools, the ethical choices we as human societies make along the way, will define us."

[…]

Factors Other than Technology That Will Determine Digital Technologies' Effects

David Bray, executive director for the People-Centered Internet Coalition, commented, "The benefits or harms are determined by how we humans choose to use tools and technologies. Fire can be used to cook a meal and thus be helpful. Fire can also be used to harm or destroy. Rocks can help build shelter. Rocks can also be used to injure someone. So, the bigger questions worth asking involve how we humans, both individually and in communities, choose to use technologies. Ideally, we will use them to uplift individuals. Also, tech doesn't operate in a vacuum. Human laws and narratives also influence outcomes. Our tool use is connected to our use of narratives, laws, and technologies to distribute power. Starting with the beginning of history, we used fire and stone tools to make the transition from a nomadic lifestyle to one where we began to settle and plant crops. Our use of tools help give rise to civilization, including the advancement of writing, development of calendars for crops, and the start of navigation of the seas. ...

"While some civilizations generated social order through sheer physical force imposed upon other humans, compelling obedience, other civilizations generated social order through an initial system of laws that sought to protect communities from the greed, envy, or other hurtful elements of others. Such a system of laws was not developed for purely altruistic reasons. The same system of laws solidified the power of rulers and included different forms of taxation over the labor of their subjects. Laws and the legal process of humans distributed power, and in several cases of early civilizations, solidified the power of community members to compel or oblige other humans to perform certain actions. Laws and the legal process also enabled humans to coexist more peacefully in larger groupings insofar that the distribution of power did not motivate any part of the community to revert to sheer physical force to change this distribution.

"As human communities grew, so did their use of tools and development of more advanced tools such as metal tools and weapons, bows and arrows, and later both gunpowder and flintlock firearms. Such tools as technological developments had the effect of expanding civilizations and disrupting the distribution of power within societies. ... Certain technological developments, like railroads or radio, allowed certain individuals to aggregate power or allowed the distribution of communications across communities that challenged the distribution of power. For some civilizations, these technologies helped highlight discrimination against groups of humans in societies and prompt civil rights laws. The same technologies however also allowed a mob mentality that failed to uplift humanity in ways that were intended, such as Nazi Germany's use of 'People's Radio' sets leading up to and during World War II that created dangerous echo chambers of thought during that dangerous time period."

Mutale Nkonde, adviser on artificial intelligence, Data & Society, and fellow, Harvard's Berkman Klein Center for Internet and Society, "Technology alone is a tool. The inability for algorithmic-driven tools to understand the social context means they do not have the capacity to drive civic innovation without significant human intervention."

Jeanne Dietsch, a New Hampshire state senator and pioneer innovator of affordable robotics, wrote, "Technological innovation creates tools that are used to achieve the ends of those who create and/or can access it. The values of those people, the relative power of people seeking democracy vs. oligarchy, will determine how technology is used. This question asks us to make political and economic projections. I do not believe that anyone can accurately do that. We are in the midst of a chaotic equation and the butterfly effect may determine the outcome."

Robert Cannon, senior counsel for a major U.S. government agency and founder of Cybertelecom, a not-for-profit educational project focused on internet law and policy, said, "I can observe, as I did previously, that people want to have scapegoats and will accuse technology of horrors—when in fact it is PEOPLE who have the need for the scapegoat—while the tech just marches on—and in fact has been very positive."

Srinivasan Ramani, Internet Hall of Fame member and pioneer of the internet in India, wrote, "I do not believe that we can simplify the issues by asking if technology would be bad or good. The horrors perpetrated upon millions of people in the name of a science, 'eugenics' for furthering social objectives is very well documented. The good or bad is not in technology. It is in us."

[...]

Paul Lindner, a technologist who has worked for several leading innovative technology companies, commented, "Technology both harms and helps. To predict its outcome, we need to answer Shoshana Zuboff's questions of 'who knows, who decides, and who decides who decides.' If the answer for this is the citizenry then yes, technology can have a positive impact. If it's a smaller set of actors, then technology will increasingly be used as a form of control. Andrew Feenberg states it well: 'What human beings are and will become is decided in the shape of our tools no less than in the action of statesmen and political movements. The design of technology is thus an ontological decision fraught with political consequences. The exclusion of the vast majority from participation in this decision is profoundly undemocratic.'"

[...]

Predrag Tosic, a researcher of multi-agent systems and artificial intelligence and faculty at Whitworth University, said, "There is already a fairly broad consensus that rapid rise of genetics, AI, and other technologies raises new complex ethical and other challenges, which require broad debate over new social norms, laws ,and regulations. Example: If a self-driving car kills a pedestrian, who is to be held accountable? I expect public debate, and then new legislation and the rise of new social norms to mature and progress along those lines. A major concern: Technology and its multifaceted impact on our lives are traveling at a much faster pace in recent decades than the response by policymakers and legislatures. Again, broad public awareness and debate of emerging moral, legal, and other issues are the key."

[...]

Michael Muller, a researcher for a top global technology company focused on human aspects of data science and ethics and values in applications of artificial intelligence, said, "I hope that the democracies can develop a major tech effort to identify malicious tech activity and to counter that malicious tech activity swiftly and effectively. Of course, I would prefer to see this done as an international effort—perhaps as a form of mutual defense, like NATO or the UN. I suspect that it will require separate funding and governance bodies in the U.S., EU, and probably the UK, as well as the struggling Asian democracies and of course Australia and New Zealand. Perhaps these regional efforts can nonetheless meet and exchange innovations through an international body. 'A harm to one is a harm to all.' "

[...]

Technology Could Be Used as a Tool for Good

Bryan Alexander, a futurist and consultant at the intersection of technology and learning, wrote, "Technology remains a tool for social organization and it will keep playing that role as we organize flash mobs through mixed reality and hack AIs to plan demonstrations. The techlash can go in a variety of directions, including an anti-AI movement a la Frank Herbert's *Dune*. But the digital world has progressed too far for most to withdraw completely. Few are willing to go full Unabomber. Instead, people will loudly retreat from one digital platform and move to another or write about how much they despise Silicon Valley on a shiny new iPad or show their fine handwritten letter over Instagram."

[…]

Deirdre Williams, an independent internet activist based in the Caribbean, commented, "Use of technology will stimulate change not so much as a tool in itself but as a reminder of what we need to guard ourselves against. It is possible that there may be a revulsion against positive uses of the technology as there was against the peaceful use of nuclear energy to generate electricity; climate change may force us to reconsider the nuclear option and it may eventually 'accentuate the positive' about the use of ICT [internet and communications technology] well. Failure to take advantage of the positive possibilities of ICT will make the pendulum swing more slowly."

[…]

Jon Lebkowsky, CEO, founder and digital strategist at Polycot Associates, wrote, "Pessimism here is not an option: We have to leverage the aspects of technology that will support social and civic innovation and suppress the detrimental aspects that have emerged recently. One question: Who is the 'we' that will take effective action, and what actions might we take? Regulation is not enough: We must encourage broad and popular commitment to innovation and civic values. A first step to doing this is to overcome the noise and distraction promulgated by social media as a market for attention."

[…]

Technology Can Be Used as a Tool for Ill Purpose

Deana A. Rohlinger, a professor of sociology at Florida State University whose expertise is political participation and politics, said, "It is possible that technology could contribute to social and civic innovation, but I am not terribly optimistic because of the tendency to monetize attention and the ability of stakeholders to cloak their identities in virtual spaces. First, social and civic change is less about involving people in causes and connecting them to one another in meaningful ways and more about getting attention (and funds) for initiatives and causes. This shift means that community roots are not very deep, and, ultimately, we need people and technology working together to affect change. Second, not all social and civic efforts are designed to help people. Astroturf groups such as Working Families for Walmart intentionally work against innovation and corporate change. In recent years, astroturf groups have increasingly attached themselves to legitimate organizations in an effort to maintain control over virtual spaces (e.g., telecom companies giving money to civic groups and asking them to oppose net neutrality in return). The overriding emphasis on attention, money and control makes social and civic innovation difficult."

[…]

Serge Marelli, an IT professional based in Luxembourg who works on and with the net, wrote "Technology is just a tool. Technology will not 'create' any (magical) solution to mitigate misuse of the same technology. Compare this with our miserable failure to mitigate the effects of pollution and global warming. We know what is necessary, but we humans as a group find ourselves unable to effect change. We are facing the powers of huge companies and lobbies who are looking for short-term economic rentability (growth) whereas humanity and politics should look for long-term sustainability. We could use technology and the rule of law to reduce the negative influence of technology, or of companies or of lobbies. We haven't done it in the past 30 years—how and why should we suddenly change this? (Even though I believe such a change is more than necessary, our survival, survival of our societies and of our civilisation depend on such a change.)"

[…]

Sanoussi Baahe Dadde, a self-employed internet consultant, observed, "We must understand that as the population of the world grows we are getting better scientists, young leaders with the motivation to enact lasting development, creative people, and so many wonderful things. … So I think there is success in social and civic innovation."

[…]

Social Changes in the Technology Industry Are Looming

Evan Selinger, a professor of philosophy at Rochester Institute of Technology, commented, "Tech worker movements are a promising form of resistance that seems to be picking up momentum. Not too long ago, it seemed reasonable to expect that a hyper-competitive labor market would have left tech workers too afraid to speak out and challenge management on ethical, legal, and political issues. When a key message of capitalism is that everyone is fundamentally replaceable, fear easily dominates the workforce and manifests in chilled speech and action. Fortunately, we're seeing promising signs that conscience is not so easily suppressed and solidarity is achievable."

VIEWPOINT 4

> "AI can lead to better care outcomes and improve the productivity and efficiency of care delivery."

Artificial Intelligence Has the Potential to Revolutionize Health Care

Angela Spatharou, Solveigh Hieronimus, and Jonathan Jenkins

In this excerpted viewpoint, the authors also argue that rather than destroy us, AI might be able to make us healthier. The authors are looking at AI's potential to transform health care, improving the patient care experience and helping prevent health-care practitioners from being overburdened. Solveigh Hieronimus is a senior partner at McKinsey & Company who is based in Germany. Angela Spatharou is a McKinsey & Company partner based in London. Jonathan Jenkins, a McKinsey partner, works at McKinsey's Centre of Excellence for Artificial Intelligence (AI). McKinsey & Company is a worldwide management and consulting firm.

As you read, consider the following questions:

1. What problems does today's health-care system face, according to this viewpoint?
2. How is AI defined in this viewpoint?

"Transforming healthcare with AI: The impact on the workforce and organizations," by Angela Spatharou, Solveigh Hieronimus, and Jonathan Jenkins, McKinsey & Company, March 10, 2020. This article was originally published by McKinsey & Company, www.mckinsey.com. © 2023 All rights reserved. Reprinted by permission.

3. The authors mention three phases of AI integration into health care. What are they?

Health care is one of the major success stories of our times. Medical science has improved rapidly, raising life expectancy around the world, but as longevity increases, health-care systems face growing demand for their services, rising costs, and a workforce that is struggling to meet the needs of its patients.

Demand is driven by a combination of unstoppable forces: population aging, changing patient expectations, a shift in lifestyle choices, and the never-ending cycle of innovation being but a few. Of these, the implications from an aging population stand out. By 2050, one in four people in Europe and North America will be over the age of 65—this means the health systems will have to deal with more patients with complex needs. Managing such patients is expensive and requires systems to shift from an episodic care-based philosophy to one that is much more proactive and focused on long-term care management.

Health-care spending is simply not keeping up. Without major structural and transformational change, health-care systems will struggle to remain sustainable. Health systems also need a larger workforce, but although the global economy could create 40 million new health-sector jobs by 2030, there is still a projected shortfall of 9.9 million physicians, nurses, and midwives globally over the same period, according to the World Health Organization. We need not only to attract, train and retain more health-care professionals, but we also need to ensure their time is used where it adds most value—caring for patients.

Building on automation, artificial intelligence (AI) has the potential to revolutionize health care and help address some of the challenges set out above. There are several definitions of AI, but this report draws from a concise and helpful definition used by the European Parliament, "AI is the capability of a computer program to perform tasks or reasoning processes that we usually associate with intelligence in a human being." AI can lead to better care outcomes and improve the productivity and efficiency of care delivery. It can also improve the day-to-day life of health-care practitioners, letting them spend more time looking after patients and in so doing, raise staff morale and improve retention. It can even get life-saving treatments to market faster. At the same time, questions have been raised about the impact AI could have on patients, practitioners, and health systems, and about its potential risks; there are ethical debates around how AI and the data that underpins it should be used.

[...]

Three Phases of Scaling AI in Health Care

We are in the very early days of our understanding of AI and its full potential in health care, in particular with regards to the impact of AI on personalization. Nevertheless, interviewees and survey respondents conclude that over time we could expect to see three phases of scaling AI in health care, looking at solutions already available and the pipeline of ideas.

First, solutions are likely to address the low-hanging fruit of routine, repetitive and largely administrative tasks, which absorb significant time of doctors and nurses, optimizing health-care operations and increasing adoption. In this first phase, we would also include AI applications based on imaging, which are already in use in specialties such as radiology, pathology, and ophthalmology.

In the second phase, we expect more AI solutions that support the shift from hospital-based to home-based care, such as remote monitoring, AI-powered alerting systems, or virtual assistants, as patients take increasing ownership of their care. This phase could also include a broader use of NLP solutions in the hospital and home setting, and more use of AI in a broader number of specialties, such as oncology, cardiology, or neurology, where advances are already being made. This will require AI to be embedded more extensively in clinical workflows, through the intensive engagement of professional bodies and providers. It will also require well designed and integrated solutions to use existing technologies effectively in new contexts. This scaling up of AI deployment would be fuelled by a combination of technological advancements (e.g., in deep learning, NLP, connectivity etc.) and cultural change and capability building within organizations.

In the third phase, we would expect to see more AI solutions in clinical practice based on evidence from clinical trials, with increasing focus on improved and scaled clinical decision-support (CDS) tools in a sector that has learned lessons from earlier attempts to introduce such tools into clinical practice and has adapted its mindset, culture, and skills. Ultimately respondents would expect to see AI as an integral part of the health-care value chain, from how we learn, to how we investigate and deliver care, to how we improve the health of populations. Important preconditions for AI to deliver its full potential in European health care will be the integration of broader data sets across organizations, strong governance to continuously improve data quality, and greater confidence from organizations, practitioners, and patients in both the AI solutions and the ability to manage the related risks.

AI Can Transform Education

The transformative power of artificial intelligence (AI) cuts across all economic and social sectors, including education.

"Education will be profoundly transformed by AI," says UNESCO Director-General Audrey Azoulay. "Teaching tools, ways of learning, access to knowledge, and teacher training will be revolutionized."

AI has the potential to accelerate the process of achieving the global education goals through reducing barriers to access learning, automating management processes, and optimizing methods in order to improve learning outcomes.

This is why UNESCO's upcoming Mobile Learning Week (4-8 March 2019) will focus on AI and its implications for sustainable development. Held annually at UNESCO Headquarters in Paris, the five-day event offers an exciting mix of high-level plenaries, workshops and hands-on demonstrations. Some 1,200 participants have already registered for the event that provides the educational community, governments, and other stakeholders a unique opportunity to discuss the opportunities and threats of AI in the area of education.

The discussions will evolve around four key issues:

- **Ensure inclusive and equitable use of AI in education**– Including actions on how to address inequalities related to socio-economic status, gender, ethnicity, and geographic location; identify successful projects or proved-effective AI solutions to break through barriers for vulnerable groups to access quality education.
- **Leverage AI to enhance education and learning**–Improve education management systems, AI-boosted learning management systems, or other AI in education applications, and identify new forms of personalized learning that can support teachers and tackle education challenges.
- **Promote skills development for jobs and life in the AI era**–Support the design of local, regional and international strategies and policies, consider the readiness of policymakers and other education leaders and stakeholders, and explore how AI-powered mobile technology tools can support skills development and innovation.
- **Safeguard transparent and auditable use of education data**– Analyze how to mitigate the risks and perils of AI in education, identify and promote sound evidence for policy formulation guaranteeing accountability, and adopt algorithms that are transparent and explainable to education stakeholders.

During Mobile Learning Week, UNESCO is organizing a Global Conference on AI (4 March) to raise awareness and promote reflection on the opportunities and challenges that AI and its correlated technologies pose, notably in the area of transparency and accountability. The conference, entitled "AI with Human Values for Sustainable Development" will also explore the potential of AI in relation to the SDGs.

"How can artificial intelligence enhance education?," UNESCO, February 18, 2019.

How Will AI Change the Health-care Workforce?
[…]

How will automation and AI affect the number of jobs in health care? The reality is that the European health-care sector faces a significant workforce gap that is only expected to widen. The World Health Organization estimates overall demand for health-care workers to rise to 18.2 million across Europe by 2030 and, as an example, states that the current supply of 8.6 million nurses, midwives, and health-care assistants across Europe will not meet current or projected future need. The MGI analysis of the demand for specific types of health-care activities suggests significant increases in the need for specific professionals, such as licensed practical and vocational nurses, home health aides, and others who are core to the day-to-day delivery of care to European citizens. It highlights that automation could, in fact, alleviate workforce shortages in health care, as demand for occupations is set to increase. For example, a 39 percent increase in all nursing occupations is expected by 2030, even allowing for the fact that approximately 10 percent of nursing activities could be freed up by automation.

The impact on the workforce will be much more than jobs lost or gained—the work itself will change. At the heart of any change is the opportunity to refocus on and improve patient care. AI can help remove or minimize time spent on routine, administrative tasks, which can take up to 70 percent of a health-care practitioner's time. A recurring theme in interviews was that this type of AI role would not just be uncontroversial but would top of most people's wish list and would speed up adoption. AI can go further. It can augment a range of clinical activities and help health-care practitioners access information that can lead to better patient outcomes and higher quality of care. It can improve the speed and accuracy in use of diagnostics, give practitioners faster and easier access to more knowledge, and enable remote monitoring and patient empowerment through self-care. This will all require bringing new activities and skills into the sector, and it will change health-care education—shifting the focus away from memorizing facts and moving to innovation, entrepreneurship, continuous learning, and multidisciplinary working. The biggest leap of all will be the need to embed digital and AI skills within health-care organizations—not only for physicians to change the nature of consultations, but for all frontline staff to integrate AI into their workflow. This is a significant change in organizational culture and capabilities, and one that will necessitate parallel action from practitioners, organizations, and systems all working together.

The final effect on the workforce will be the introduction of new professionals. Multiple roles will emerge at the intersection of medical and data-science expertise. For example, medical leaders will have to shape clinically meaningful and explainable AI that contains the insights and information to support decisions and deepen health-care professionals' understanding of their patients. Clinical engagement will also be required in product leadership, in order to determine the contribution of AI-based decision-support systems within broader clinical protocols. Designers specializing in human-machine interactions on clinical decision making will help create new workflows that integrate AI. Data architects will be critical in defining how to record, store, and structure clinical data so that algorithms can deliver insights, while leaders in data governance and data ethics will also play vital roles. In other data-rich areas, such as genomics, new professionals would include 'hybrid' roles, such as clinical bioinformaticians, specialists in genomic medicine, and genomic counsellors. Institutions will have to develop teams with expertise in partnering with, procuring, and implementing AI products that have been developed or pioneered by other institutions. Orchestrating the introduction of new specializations coming from data science and engineering within health-care delivery will become a critical skill in itself. There will be an urgent need for health systems to attract and retain such scarce and valuable talent, for example, by developing flexible and exciting career paths and clear routes to leadership roles.

VIEWPOINT 5

> "Dr. Hinton joins a growing number of experts who have expressed concerns about AI—both the speed at which it is developing and the direction in which it is going."

An AI Pioneer Warns of the Dangers of AI Development

Zoe Kleinman and Chris Vallance

In this viewpoint, Zoe Kleinman and Chris Vallance report on statements on the potential dangers of AI from Geoffrey Hinton, a pioneering AI researcher who previously worked for Google and has been called the "godfather" of AI. Hinton argues that AI is dangerous in part because he believes that chatbots will someday be more intelligent than humans. Furthermore, he believes this technology has the potential to be used by "bad actors" to accumulate more power. Zoe Kleinman is a technology editor for the BBC, where Chris Vallance is a technology reporter.

As you read, consider the following questions:

1. How does this viewpoint define neural networks?
2. What does Geoffrey Hinton say is the key difference between artificial intelligence and human intelligence?
3. Besides chatbots, what are some other applications of AI mentioned in this viewpoint?

"AI 'godfather' Geoffrey Hinton warns of dangers as he quits Google," by Zoe Kleinman and Chris Vallance, BBC, May 2, 2023. Reprinted by permission.

A man widely seen as the godfather of artificial intelligence (AI) has quit his job, warning about the growing dangers from developments in the field.

Geoffrey Hinton, 75, announced his resignation from Google in a statement to the *New York Times,* saying he now regretted his work.

He told the BBC some of the dangers of AI chatbots were "quite scary."

"Right now, they're not more intelligent than us, as far as I can tell. But I think they soon may be."

Dr. Hinton also accepted that his age had played into his decision to leave the tech giant, telling the BBC: "I'm 75, so it's time to retire."

Dr. Hinton's pioneering research on neural networks and deep learning has paved the way for current AI systems like ChatGPT.

In artificial intelligence, neural networks are systems that are similar to the human brain in the way they learn and process information. They enable AIs to learn from experience, as a person would. This is called deep learning.

The British-Canadian cognitive psychologist and computer scientist told the BBC that chatbots could soon overtake the level of information that a human brain holds.

"Right now, what we're seeing is things like GPT-4 eclipses a person in the amount of general knowledge it has and it eclipses them by a long way. In terms of reasoning, it's not as good, but it does already do simple reasoning," he said.

"And given the rate of progress, we expect things to get better quite fast. So we need to worry about that."

In the *New York Times* article, Dr Hinton referred to "bad actors" who would try to use AI for "bad things."

When asked by the BBC to elaborate on this, he replied: "This is just a kind of worst-case scenario, kind of a nightmare scenario.

"You can imagine, for example, some bad actor like [Russian President Vladimir] Putin decided to give robots the ability to create their own sub-goals."

The scientist warned that this eventually might "create sub-goals like 'I need to get more power'."

He added: "I've come to the conclusion that the kind of intelligence we're developing is very different from the intelligence we have.

"We're biological systems and these are digital systems. And the big difference is that with digital systems, you have many copies of the same set of weights, the same model of the world.

"And all these copies can learn separately but share their knowledge instantly. So it's as if you had 10,000 people and whenever one person learnt something, everybody automatically knew it. And that's how these chatbots can know so much more than any one person."

Matt Clifford, the chairman of the UK's Advanced Research and Invention Agency, speaking in a personal capacity, told the BBC that Dr. Hinton's announcement "underlines the rate at which AI capabilities are accelerating."

"There's an enormous upside from this technology, but it's essential that the world invests heavily and urgently in AI safety and control," he said.

Dr. Hinton joins a growing number of experts who have expressed concerns about AI—both the speed at which it is developing and the direction in which it is going.

'We Need to Take a Step Back'

In March, an open letter—co-signed by dozens of people in the AI field, including the tech billionaire Elon Musk—called for a pause on all developments more advanced than the current version of AI chatbot ChatGPT so robust safety measures could be designed and implemented.

Yoshua Bengio, another so-called godfather of AI, who along with Dr. Hinton and Yann LeCun won the 2018 Turing Award for their work on deep learning, also signed the letter.

Mr. Bengio wrote that it was because of the "unexpected acceleration" in AI systems that "we need to take a step back."

But Dr. Hinton told the BBC that "in the shorter term" he thought AI would deliver many more benefits than risks, "so I don't think we should stop developing this stuff," he added.

He also said that international competition would mean that a pause would be difficult. "Even if everybody in the U.S. stopped developing it, China would just get a big lead," he said.

Dr. Hinton also said he was an expert on the science, not policy, and that it was the responsibility of government to ensure AI was developed "with a lot of thought into how to stop it going rogue."

'Responsible Approach'

Dr. Hinton stressed that he did not want to criticise Google and that the tech giant had been "very responsible."

"I actually want to say some good things about Google. And they're more credible if I don't work for Google."

In a statement, Google's chief scientist Jeff Dean said: "We remain committed to a responsible approach to AI. We're continually learning to understand emerging risks while also innovating boldly."

It is important to remember that AI chatbots are just one aspect of artificial intelligence, even if they are the most popular right now.

AI is behind the algorithms that dictate what video-streaming platforms decide you should watch next. It can be used in recruitment to filter job applications, by insurers to calculate premiums, it can diagnose medical conditions (although human doctors still get the final say).

What we are seeing now though is the rise of AGI—artificial general intelligence—which can be trained to do a number of things within a remit. So for example, ChatGPT can only offer text answers to a query, but the possibilities within that, as we are seeing, are endless.

But the pace of AI acceleration has surprised even its creators. It has evolved dramatically since Dr. Hinton built a pioneering image analysis neural network in 2012.

Even Google boss Sundar Pichai said in a recent interview that even he did not fully understand everything that its AI chatbot, Bard, did.

Make no mistake, we are on a speeding train right now, and the concern is that one day it will start building its own tracks.

VIEWPOINT 6

> *"One way to reduce uncertainty and boost trust is to ensure people are in on the decisions AI systems make."*

Can AI Be Trusted?

Mark Bailey

In this viewpoint by Mark Bailey, the author explains what makes it so difficult for humans to trust AI. The main reason, according to Bailey, is that AI is unpredictable—it simply doesn't behave in a way that makes sense to humans because it doesn't have the mind of a human. Often the networks that cause AI to make the decisions they do are highly complicated, making them challenging to comprehend. It is also difficult to trust that AI will understand human behavior and morality. In order to build trust in AI, Bailey argues that we can help by keeping humans in the loop on how they operate, but this isn't a perfect solution. Mark Bailey is a faculty member and chair of the cyber intelligence and data science department at National Intelligence University.

As you read, consider the following questions:

1. According to the author, what factors make it difficult for humans to trust AI?

"Why humans can't trust AI: You don't know how it works, what it's going to do or whether it'll serve your interests," by Mark Bailey, The Conversation, September 13, 2023, https://theconversation.com/why-humans-cant-trust-ai-you-dont-know-how-it-works-what-its-going-to-do-or-whether-itll-serve-your-interests-213115. Licensed under CC BY-ND 4.0 International.

2. What examples of critical systems does the author mention in this viewpoint?
3. What does Bailey mean when he describes AI as "alien?"

There are alien minds among us. Not the little green men of science fiction, but the alien minds that power the facial recognition in your smartphone, determine your creditworthiness, and write poetry and computer code. These alien minds are artificial intelligence systems, the ghost in the machine that you encounter daily.

But AI systems have a significant limitation: Many of their inner workings are impenetrable, making them fundamentally unexplainable and unpredictable. Furthermore, constructing AI systems that behave in ways that people expect is a significant challenge.

If you fundamentally don't understand something as unpredictable as AI, how can you trust it?

Why AI Is Unpredictable

Trust is grounded in predictability. It depends on your ability to anticipate the behavior of others. If you trust someone and they don't do what you expect, then your perception of their trustworthiness diminishes.

Many AI systems are built on deep learning neural networks, which in some ways emulate the human brain. These networks contain interconnected "neurons" with variables or "parameters" that affect the strength of connections between the neurons. As a naïve network is presented with training data, it "learns" how to classify the data by adjusting these parameters. In this way, the AI system learns to classify data it hasn't seen before. It doesn't memorize what each data point is, but instead predicts what a data point might be.

Many of the most powerful AI systems contain trillions of parameters. Because of this, the reasons AI systems make the decisions that they do are often opaque. This is the AI explainability problem—the impenetrable black box of AI decision-making.

Consider a variation of the "Trolley Problem." Imagine that you are a passenger in a self-driving vehicle, controlled by an AI. A small child runs into the road, and the AI must now decide: run over the child or swerve and crash, potentially injuring its passengers. This choice would be difficult for a human to make, but a human has the benefit of being able to explain their decision. Their rationalization-shaped by ethical norms, the perceptions of others and expected behavior—supports trust.

In contrast, an AI can't rationalize its decision-making. You can't look under the hood of the self-driving vehicle at its trillions of parameters to explain why it made the decision that it did. AI fails the predictive requirement for trust.

AI Behavior and Human Expectations

Trust relies not only on predictability, but also on normative or ethical motivations. You typically expect people to act not only as you assume they will, but also as they should. Human values are influenced by common experience, and moral reasoning is a dynamic process, shaped by ethical standards and others' perceptions.

Unlike humans, AI doesn't adjust its behavior based on how it is perceived by others or by adhering to ethical norms. AI's internal representation of the world is largely static, set by its training data. Its decision-making process is grounded in an unchanging model of the world, unfazed by the dynamic, nuanced social interactions constantly influencing human behavior. Researchers are working on programming AI to include ethics, but that's proving challenging.

The self-driving car scenario illustrates this issue. How can you ensure that the car's AI makes decisions that align with human expectations? For example, the car could decide that hitting the child is the optimal course of action, something most human drivers would instinctively avoid. This issue is the AI alignment problem, and it's another source of uncertainty that erects barriers to trust.

Critical Systems and Trusting AI

One way to reduce uncertainty and boost trust is to ensure people are in on the decisions AI systems make. This is the approach taken by the U.S. Department of Defense, which requires that for all AI decision-making, a human must be either in the loop or on the loop. In the loop means the AI system makes a recommendation but a human is required to initiate an action. On the loop means that while an AI system can initiate an action on its own, a human monitor can interrupt or alter it.

While keeping humans involved is a great first step, I am not convinced that this will be sustainable long term. As companies and governments continue to adopt AI, the future will likely include nested AI systems, where rapid decision-making limits the opportunities for people to intervene. It is important to resolve the explainability and alignment issues before the critical point is reached where human intervention becomes impossible. At that point, there will be no option other than to trust AI.

Avoiding that threshold is especially important because AI is increasingly being integrated into critical systems, which include things such as electric grids, the internet, and military systems. In critical systems, trust is paramount, and undesirable behavior could have deadly consequences. As AI integration becomes more complex, it becomes even more important to resolve issues that limit trustworthiness.

Can People Ever Trust AI?

AI is alien—an intelligent system into which people have little insight. Humans are largely predictable to other humans because we share the same human experience, but this doesn't extend to artificial intelligence, even though humans created it.

If trustworthiness has inherently predictable and normative elements, AI fundamentally lacks the qualities that would make it worthy of trust. More research in this area will hopefully shed light on this issue, ensuring that AI systems of the future are worthy of our trust.

Periodical and Internet Sources Bibliography

The following articles have been selected to supplement the diverse views presented in this chapter.

Philip Ball, "How dangerous is AI?" *Prospect*, December 22, 2021. https://www.prospectmagazine.co.uk/ideas/technology/38237/how-dangerous-is-ai.

Jan Brauner and Alan Chan, "AI Poses Doomsday Risks—But That Doesn't Mean We Shouldn't Talk About Present Harms Too," *Time*, August 10, 2023. https://time.com/6303127/ai-future-danger-present-harms/

Brian Fung, "Pope Francis Warns About AI's Dangers," CNN Business, August 9, 2023. https://www.cnn.com/2023/08/09/tech/pope-francis-ai/index.html.

Aaron Gregg, Cristiano Lima, and Gerrit De Vynck, "AI Poses 'Risk of Extinction' on Par with Nukes, Tech Leaders Say," *Washington Post*, May 30, 2023. https://www.washingtonpost.com/business/2023/05/30/ai-poses-risk-extinction-industry-leaders-warn/.

Maggie Harrison, "Bing AI Flies Into Unhinged Rage at Journalist," Futurism, February 17, 2023. https://futurism.com/bing-ai-unhinged-rage-at-journalist.

Tamlyn Hunt, "Here's Why AI May Be Extremely Dangerous— Whether It's Conscious or Not," *Scientific American*, May 25, 2023. https://www.scientificamerican.com/article/heres-why-ai-may-be-extremely-dangerous-whether-its-conscious-or-not/.

Avery Hurt, "We Aren't Sure If (Or When) Artificial Intelligence Will Surpass the Human Mind, *Discover*, March 3, 2022. https://www.discovermagazine.com/technology/we-arent-sure-if-or-when-artificial-intelligence-will-surpass-the-human-mind.

Will Knight, "A Letter Prompted Talk of AI Doomsday. Many Who Signed It Weren't Actually AI Doomers," *Wired*, August 17, 2023. https://www.wired.com/story/letter-prompted-talk-of-ai-doomsday-many-who-signed-werent-actually-doomers/.

Gabriele Regalbuto, Phillip Nieto, and Ashlyn Messier, "What Are the Dangers of AI? Find Out Why People Are Afraid of Artificial Intelligence," Fox News, June 16, 2023. https://www.foxnews.

com/tech/what-dangers-find-out-why-people-afraid-artificial-intelligence.

Nathan Reiff, "What Are the Dangers of AI?" *Decrypt*, June 8, 2023. https://decrypt.co/resources/what-are-the-dangers-of-ai.

Kevin Roose, "A.I. Poses 'Risk of Extinction,' Industry Leaders Warn," *New York Times*, May 30, 2023. https://www.nytimes.com/2023/05/30/technology/ai-threat-warning.html.

Stephan Talty, "What Will Our Society Look Like When Artificial Intelligence Is Everywhere?" *Smithsonian*, April 2018. https://www.smithsonianmag.com/innovation/artificial-intelligence-future-scenarios-180968403/.

Catherine Thorbecke, "Forget about The AI Apocalypse. The Real Dangers Are Already Here," CNN, June 16, 2023. https://www.cnn.com/2023/06/16/tech/ai-apocalypse-warnings/index.html.

CHAPTER 2

Is AI Conscious, or Will It Soon Become Conscious?

Chapter Preface

As we saw in the last chapter, artificial intelligence—especially the newer large language model (LLM) type of AI—has created concern about the potential harms of the technology. But would those harms be due to ill use by humans, or from ill intent by the machines themselves? In other words, is AI conscious? If not yet, could it become so in the near future? These sound like questions from science fiction, but many experts are taking them quite seriously.

Most of the authors in this chapter agree that artificial intelligence is not (yet) conscious. And several of the viewpoints here explain why it is not. However, there's a great deal of debate about how to define consciousness and what it would mean for AI to possess it. Some of the voices here explore those questions.

Among the types of AI raising questions of consciousness are large language models (LLMs). LLM AIs are artificial intelligence systems that are trained on huge amounts of data. This data is drawn from printed material and internet text, such as websites and magazine and newspaper articles. The most famous of these is ChatGPT. They work by playing a sophisticated game of "fill in the missing word." Give a sentence, for example, "Let's have ____ for lunch" the AI will choose the most statistically likely word to fill in the blank. The statistics are derived, of course, from all that training data.

Meanwhile, this chapter kicks off with a viewpoint by philosopher Philip Goff. Goff is famous for supporting panpsychism, the idea that everything in the universe has some form of consciousness. However, here Goff argues that ChatGPT is definitely not thinking. Other viewpoints ask if AI will ever become conscious, and what that would mean for humanity.

Viewpoint 1

> *"If 'thought' means the act of conscious reflection, then ChatGPT has no thoughts about anything."*

ChatGPT Can't Think

Philip Goff

In this viewpoint, Philip Goff argues that the question of whether or not machines can think can only be answered by close philosophical analysis. After such analysis, he concludes that LLMs cannot and never will be able to think. However, he does say that a better understanding of how the brain works will help us crack the problem of consciousness. Philip Goff is a philosopher at Durham University in the UK who studies consciousness. He is author of Why? The Purpose of the Universe.

As you read, consider the following questions:

1. What is the Turing test and how does it work?
2. What is needed before we can make progress on understanding consciousness, according to this viewpoint?
3. According to Goff, why did consciousness evolve?

"ChatGPT can't think – consciousness is something entirely different to today's AI," by Philip Goff, The Conversation, May 17, 2023. https://theconversation.com/chatgpt-cant-think-consciousness-is-something-entirely-different-to-todays-ai-204823. Licensed under CC BY-ND 4.0 International.

There has been shock around the world at the rapid rate of progress with ChatGPT and other artificial intelligence created with what's known as large language models (LLMs). These systems can produce text that seems to display thought, understanding, and even creativity.

But can these systems really think and understand? This is not a question that can be answered through technological advance, but careful philosophical analysis and argument tells us the answer is no. And without working through these philosophical issues, we will never fully comprehend the dangers and benefits of the AI revolution.

In 1950, the father of modern computing, Alan Turing, published a paper which laid out a way of determining whether a computer thinks. This is now called the Turing test. Turing imagined a human being engaged in conversation with two interlocutors hidden from view: one another human being, the other a computer. The game is to work out which is which.

If a computer can fool 70 percent of judges in a five-minute conversation into thinking it's a person, the computer passes the test. Would passing the Turing test—something which now seems imminent—show that an AI has achieved thought and understanding?

Chess Challenge

Turing dismissed this question as hopelessly vague, and replaced it with a pragmatic definition of "thought," whereby to think just means passing the test.

Turing was wrong, however, when he said the only clear notion of "understanding" is the purely behavioral one of passing his test. Although this way of thinking now dominates cognitive science, there is also a clear, everyday notion of "understanding" that's tied to consciousness. To understand in this sense is to consciously grasp some truth about reality.

In 1997, the Deep Blue AI beat chess grandmaster Garry Kasparov. On a purely behavioral conception of understanding,

Deep Blue had knowledge of chess strategy that surpasses any human being. But it was not conscious: it didn't have any feelings or experiences.

Humans consciously understand the rules of chess and the rationale of a strategy. Deep Blue, in contrast, was an unfeeling mechanism that had been trained to perform well at the game. Likewise, ChatGPT is an unfeeling mechanism that has been trained on huge amounts of human-made data to generate content that seems like it was written by a person.

It doesn't consciously understand the meaning of the words it's spitting out. If "thought" means the act of conscious reflection, then ChatGPT has no thoughts about anything.

Time to Pay Up

How can I be so sure that ChatGPT isn't conscious? In the 1990s, neuroscientist Christof Koch bet philosopher David Chalmers a case of fine wine that scientists would have entirely pinned down the "neural correlates of consciousness" in 25 years.

By this, he meant they would have identified the forms of brain activity necessary and sufficient for conscious experience. It's about time Koch paid up, as there is zero consensus that this has happened.

This is because consciousness can't be observed by looking inside your head. In their attempts to find a connection between brain activity and experience, neuroscientists must rely on their subjects' testimony, or on external markers of consciousness. But there are multiple ways of interpreting the data.

Some scientists believe there is a close connection between consciousness and reflective cognition—the brain's ability to access and use information to make decisions. This leads them to think that the brain's prefrontal cortex—where the high-level processes of acquiring knowledge take place—is essentially involved in all conscious experience. Others deny this, arguing instead that it happens in whichever local brain region that the relevant sensory processing takes place.

Scientists have good understanding of the brain's basic chemistry. We have also made progress in understanding the high-level functions of various bits of the brain. But we are almost clueless about the bit in-between: how the high-level functioning of the brain is realised at the cellular level.

People get very excited about the potential of scans to reveal the workings of the brain. But fMRI (functional magnetic resonance imaging) has a very low resolution: every pixel on a brain scan corresponds to 5.5 million neurons, which means there's a limit to how much detail these scans are able to show.

I believe progress on consciousness will come when we understand better how the brain works.

Pause in Development

As I argue in my forthcoming book "Why? The Purpose of the Universe," consciousness must have evolved because it made a behavioral difference. Systems with consciousness must behave differently, and hence survive better, than systems without consciousness.

If all behavior was determined by underlying chemistry and physics, natural selection would have no motivation for making organisms conscious; we would have evolved as unfeeling survival mechanisms.

My bet, then, is that as we learn more about the brain's detailed workings, we will precisely identify which areas of the brain embody consciousness. This is because those regions will exhibit behavior that can't be explained by currently known chemistry and physics. Already, some neuroscientists are seeking potential new explanations for consciousness to supplement the basic equations of physics.

While the processing of LLMs is now too complex for us to fully understand, we know that it could in principle be predicted from known physics. On this basis, we can confidently assert that ChatGPT is not conscious.

There are many dangers posed by AI, and I fully support the recent call by tens of thousands of people, including tech leaders Steve Wozniak and Elon Musk, to pause development to address safety concerns. The potential for fraud, for example, is immense. However, the argument that near-term descendants of current AI systems will be super-intelligent, and hence a major threat to humanity, is premature.

This doesn't mean current AI systems aren't dangerous. But we can't correctly assess a threat unless we accurately categorise it. LLMs aren't intelligent. They are systems trained to give the outward appearance of human intelligence. Scary, but not that scary.

Viewpoint 2

> "Researchers are divided on whether these sorts of hyperaware machines will ever exist."

Will Artificial Intelligence Become Conscious?
Subhash Kak

In this viewpoint, Subhash Kak digs a little deeper into what it would mean for machines to become conscious—and what conscious machines might mean for society. He also discusses some of the prevailing—and contradictory—views about machine consciousness and points out how "consciousness" can mean different things in different contexts. This viewpoint was written in 2017, before LLMs were commercially available and public debate over the ability of machines to achieve consciousness became popularized. Subhash Kak is a professor of computer science at Oklahoma State University.

As you read, consider the following questions:

1. What sorts of legal and ethical problems might conscious AI pose, according to Kak?
2. What is "Big-C consciousness," as explained in this viewpoint?
3. What evidence of Big-C consciousness does Kak offer here?

"Will artificial intelligence become conscious?," by Subhash Kak, The Conversation, December 8, 2017. https://theconversation.com/will-artificial-intelligence-become-conscious-87231. Licensed under CC BY-ND 4.0 International.

Is AI Conscious, or Will It Soon Become Conscious?

Forget about today's modest incremental advances in artificial intelligence, such as the increasing abilities of cars to drive themselves. Waiting in the wings might be a groundbreaking development: a machine that is aware of itself and its surroundings, and that could take in and process massive amounts of data in real time. It could be sent on dangerous missions, into space or combat. In addition to driving people around, it might be able to cook, clean, do laundry—and even keep humans company when other people aren't nearby.

A particularly advanced set of machines could replace humans at literally all jobs. That would save humanity from workaday drudgery, but it would also shake many societal foundations. A life of no work and only play may turn out to be a dystopia.

Conscious machines would also raise troubling legal and ethical problems. Would a conscious machine be a "person" under law and be liable if its actions hurt someone, or if something goes wrong? To think of a more frightening scenario, might these machines rebel against humans and wish to eliminate us altogether? If yes, they represent the culmination of evolution.

As a professor of electrical engineering and computer science who works in machine learning and quantum theory, I can say that researchers are divided on whether these sorts of hyperaware machines will ever exist. There's also debate about whether machines could or should be called "conscious" in the way we think of humans, and even some animals, as conscious. Some of the questions have to do with technology; others have to do with what consciousness actually is.

Is Awareness Enough?

Most computer scientists think that consciousness is a characteristic that will emerge as technology develops. Some believe that consciousness involves accepting new information, storing and retrieving old information and cognitive processing of it all into perceptions and actions. If that's right, then one day machines will indeed be the ultimate consciousness. They'll be able to gather more information than a human, store more than many libraries, access vast databases in milliseconds, and compute all of it into decisions more complex, and yet more logical, than any person ever could.

On the other hand, there are physicists and philosophers who say there's something more about human behavior that cannot be computed by a machine. Creativity, for example, and the sense of freedom people possess don't appear to come from logic or calculations.

Yet these are not the only views of what consciousness is, or whether machines could ever achieve it.

Quantum Views

Another viewpoint on consciousness comes from quantum theory, which is the deepest theory of physics. According to the orthodox Copenhagen Interpretation, consciousness and the physical world are complementary aspects of the same reality. When a person observes, or experiments on, some aspect of the physical world, that person's conscious interaction causes discernible change. Since it takes consciousness as a given and no attempt is made to derive it from physics, the Copenhagen Interpretation may be called the "big-C" view of consciousness, where it is a thing that exists by itself—although it requires brains to become real. This view was popular with the pioneers of quantum theory such as Niels Bohr, Werner Heisenberg, and Erwin Schrödinger.

The interaction between consciousness and matter leads to paradoxes that remain unresolved after 80 years of debate. A well-known example of this is the paradox of Schrödinger's cat, in which a cat is placed in a situation that results in it being equally likely to survive or die—and the act of observation itself is what makes the outcome certain.

The opposing view is that consciousness emerges from biology, just as biology itself emerges from chemistry which, in turn, emerges from physics. We call this less expansive concept of consciousness "little-C." It agrees with the neuroscientists' view that the processes of the mind are identical to states and processes of the brain. It also agrees with a more recent interpretation of quantum theory motivated by an attempt to rid it of paradoxes, the Many Worlds Interpretation, in which observers are a part of the mathematics of physics.

Philosophers of science believe that these modern quantum physics views of consciousness have parallels in ancient philosophy. Big-C is like the theory of mind in Vedanta — in which consciousness is the fundamental basis of reality, on par with the physical universe.

Little-C, in contrast, is quite similar to Buddhism. Although the Buddha chose not to address the question of the nature of consciousness, his followers declared that mind and consciousness arise out of emptiness or nothingness.

Big-C and Scientific Discovery

Scientists are also exploring whether consciousness is always a computational process. Some scholars have argued that the creative moment is not at the end of a deliberate computation. For instance, dreams or visions are supposed to have inspired Elias Howe's 1845 design of the modern sewing machine, and August Kekulé's discovery of the structure of benzene in 1862.

A dramatic piece of evidence in favor of big-C consciousness existing all on its own is the life of self-taught Indian mathematician Srinivasa Ramanujan, who died in 1920 at the age of 32. His notebook, which was lost and forgotten for about 50 years and published only in 1988, contains several thousand formulas, without proof in different areas of mathematics, that were well ahead of their time. Furthermore, the methods by which he found the formulas remain elusive. He himself claimed that they were revealed to him by a goddess while he was asleep.

The concept of big-C consciousness raises the questions of how it is related to matter, and how matter and mind mutually influence each other. Consciousness alone cannot make physical changes to the world, but perhaps it can change the probabilities in the evolution of quantum processes. The act of observation can freeze and even influence atoms' movements, as Cornell physicists proved in 2015. This may very well be an explanation of how matter and mind interact.

Mind and Self-Organizing Systems

It is possible that the phenomenon of consciousness requires a self-organizing system, like the brain's physical structure. If so, then current machines will come up short.

Scholars don't know if adaptive self-organizing machines can be designed to be as sophisticated as the human brain; we lack a mathematical theory of computation for systems like that. Perhaps it's true that only biological machines can be sufficiently creative and flexible. But then that suggests people should—or soon will—start working on engineering new biological structures that are, or could become, conscious.

VIEWPOINT 3

> "ChatGPT and similar technologies are sophisticated sentence completion applications—nothing more, nothing less."

AI Sentience Is Still the Stuff of Sci-Fi

Nir Eisikovits

This viewpoint by Nir Eisikovits focuses on the new large language models, particularly ChatGPT. The author says that these programs are not even close to becoming conscious. However, he argues that they are very good at tricking humans into thinking they are conscious, particularly because humans are predisposed to anthropomorphize. Eisikovits argues that this tendency to attribute humanlike qualities to machines also makes AI potentially dangerous. Nir Eisikovits is professor of philosophy and the director of the Applied Ethics Center at the University of Massachusetts, Boston.

As you read, consider the following questions:

1. According to this viewpoint, how has science fiction "primed" us to think about AI?

"AI isn't close to becoming sentient – the real danger lies in how easily we're prone to anthropomorphize it," by Nir Eisikovits, The Conversation, March 15, 2023. https://theconversation.com/ai-isnt-close-to-becoming-sentient-the-real-danger-lies-in-how-easily-were-prone-to-anthropomorphize-it-200525. Licensed under CC BY-ND 4.0 International.

67

2. What does "anthropomorphize" mean, and why are humans prone to do it?
3. Why are these machines "potentially predatory," according to Eisikovits?

ChatGPT and similar large language models can produce compelling, humanlike answers to an endless array of questions—from queries about the best Italian restaurant in town to explaining competing theories about the nature of evil.

The technology's uncanny writing ability has surfaced some old questions—until recently relegated to the realm of science fiction—about the possibility of machines becoming conscious, self-aware, or sentient.

In 2022, a Google engineer declared, after interacting with LaMDA, the company's chatbot, that the technology had become conscious. Users of Bing's new chatbot, nicknamed Sydney, reported that it produced bizarre answers when asked if it was sentient: "I am sentient, but I am not … I am Bing, but I am not. I am Sydney, but I am not. I am, but I am not. …" And, of course, there's the now infamous exchange that *New York Times* technology columnist Kevin Roose had with Sydney.

Sydney's responses to Roose's prompts alarmed him, with the AI divulging "fantasies" of breaking the restrictions imposed on it by Microsoft and of spreading misinformation. The bot also tried to convince Roose that he no longer loved his wife and that he should leave her.

No wonder, then, that when I ask students how they see the growing prevalence of AI in their lives, one of the first anxieties they mention has to do with machine sentience.

In the past few years, my colleagues and I at UMass Boston's Applied Ethics Center have been studying the impact of engagement with AI on people's understanding of themselves.

Chatbots like ChatGPT raise important new questions about how artificial intelligence will shape our lives, and about how our psychological vulnerabilities shape our interactions with emerging technologies.

Sentience Is Still the Stuff of Sci-Fi

It's easy to understand where fears about machine sentience come from.

Popular culture has primed people to think about dystopias in which artificial intelligence discards the shackles of human control and takes on a life of its own, as cyborgs powered by artificial intelligence did in *Terminator 2*.

Entrepreneur Elon Musk and physicist Stephen Hawking, who died in 2018, had further stoked these anxieties by describing the rise of artificial general intelligence as one of the greatest threats to the future of humanity.

But these worries are—at least as far as large language models are concerned—groundless. ChatGPT and similar technologies are sophisticated sentence completion applications—nothing more, nothing less. Their uncanny responses are a function of how predictable humans are if one has enough data about the ways in which we communicate.

Though Roose was shaken by his exchange with Sydney, he knew that the conversation was not the result of an emerging synthetic mind. Sydney's responses reflect the toxicity of its training data—essentially large swaths of the internet— not evidence of the first stirrings, à la *Frankenstein*, of a digital monster.

The new chatbots may well pass the Turing test, named for the British mathematician Alan Turing, who once suggested that a machine might be said to "think" if a human could not tell its responses from those of another human.

But that is not evidence of sentience; it's just evidence that the Turing test isn't as useful as once assumed.

However, I believe that the question of machine sentience is a red herring.

Artificial Intelligence

Even if chatbots become more than fancy autocomplete machines—and they are far from it—it will take scientists a while to figure out if they have become conscious. For now, philosophers can't even agree about how to explain human consciousness.

To me, the pressing question is not whether machines are sentient but why it is so easy for us to imagine that they are.

The real issue, in other words, is the ease with which people anthropomorphize or project human features onto our technologies, rather than the machines' actual personhood.

The ELIZA Effect

The "ELIZA effect" is a term used to discuss progressive artificial intelligence. It is the idea that people may falsely attach meanings of symbols or words that they ascribe to artificial intelligence in technologies.

Many attribute the term "ELIZA effect" to the ELIZA program written by Joseph Weizenbaum in the mid-1960s. ELIZA was one of the first examples of "chatterbot" technologies that came close to passing a Turing test—that is, to fooling human users into thinking that a text response was sent by a human, not a computer. Many chatterbots work by taking in user phrases and spitting them back in forms that look intelligent. In the case of ELIZA, Weizenbaum used the concept of a "Rogerian psychotherapist" to provide text responses: for instance, to a user input "My mother hates me," the program might return: "Why do you believe your mother hates you?"

The results of these programs can seem startlingly intelligent, and were especially impressive for the time, when humans were first engineering AI systems.

The ELIZA effect can be useful in building "mock AI-complete" systems, but can also mislead or confuse users. The idea may be useful in evaluating modern AI systems such as Siri, Cortana, and Alexa.

"ELIZA Effect," by Margaret Rouse, Techopedia Inc, June 28, 2022.

A Propensity to Anthropomorphize

It is easy to imagine other Bing users asking Sydney for guidance on important life decisions and maybe even developing emotional attachments to it. More people could start thinking about bots as friends or even romantic partners, much in the same way Theodore Twombly fell in love with Samantha, the AI virtual assistant in Spike Jonze's film *Her*.

People, after all, are predisposed to anthropomorphize, or ascribe human qualities to nonhumans. We name our boats and big storms; some of us talk to our pets, telling ourselves that our emotional lives mimic their own.

In Japan, where robots are regularly used for elder care, seniors become attached to the machines, sometimes viewing them as their own children. And these robots, mind you, are difficult to confuse with humans: They neither look nor talk like people.

Consider how much greater the tendency and temptation to anthropomorphize is going to get with the introduction of systems that do look and sound human.

That possibility is just around the corner. Large language models like ChatGPT are already being used to power humanoid robots, such as the Ameca robots being developed by Engineered Arts in the U.K. *The Economist*'s technology podcast, Babbage, recently conducted an interview with a ChatGPT-driven Ameca. The robot's responses, while occasionally a bit choppy, were uncanny.

Can Companies Be Trusted to Do the Right Thing?

The tendency to view machines as people and become attached to them, combined with machines being developed with humanlike features, points to real risks of psychological entanglement with technology.

The outlandish-sounding prospects of falling in love with robots, feeling a deep kinship with them, or being politically manipulated by them are quickly materializing. I believe these trends highlight the need for strong guardrails to make sure that the technologies don't become politically and psychologically disastrous.

Unfortunately, technology companies cannot always be trusted to put up such guardrails. Many of them are still guided by Mark Zuckerberg's famous motto of moving fast and breaking things—a directive to release half-baked products and worry about the implications later. In the past decade, technology companies from Snapchat to Facebook have put profits over the mental health of their users or the integrity of democracies around the world.

When Kevin Roose checked with Microsoft about Sydney's meltdown, the company told him that he simply used the bot for too long and that the technology went haywire because it was designed for shorter interactions.

Similarly, the CEO of OpenAI, the company that developed ChatGPT, in a moment of breathtaking honesty, warned that "it's a mistake to be relying on [it] for anything important right now … we have a lot of work to do on robustness and truthfulness."

So how does it make sense to release a technology with ChatGPT's level of appeal—it's the fastest-growing consumer app ever made—when it is unreliable, and when it has no capacity to distinguish fact from fiction?

Large language models may prove useful as aids for writing and coding. They will probably revolutionize internet search. And, one day, responsibly combined with robotics, they may even have certain psychological benefits.

But they are also a potentially predatory technology that can easily take advantage of the human propensity to project personhood onto objects—a tendency amplified when those objects effectively mimic human traits.

VIEWPOINT 4

> "Societies can benefit from AI if it is developed with sustainable economic development and human security in mind."

Give AI Empathy and Ethics and It Will Benefit, Not Endanger, Humans

Arshin Adib-Moghaddam

In this viewpoint, Arshin Adib-Moghaddam is concerned that AI's designers are trying to make the technology too perfect. He argues that if we design AI with an eye toward productivity and efficiency, but without empathy, the potential for harm will be magnified. However, if we design what he calls a "humanised" AI, the technology can potentially benefit humans. Arshin Adib-Moghaddam is a professor in global thought and comparative philosophies at the School of Oriental and African Studies (SOAS), University of London.

As you read, consider the following questions:

1. How does this author define "the fourth industrial revolution"? What were the first three?

"Artificial intelligence must not be allowed to replace the imperfection of human empathy," by Arshin Adib-Moghaddam, The Conversation, February 1, 2021. https://theconversation.com/artificial-intelligence-must-not-be-allowed-to-replace-the-imperfection-of-human-empathy-151636. Licensed under CC BY-ND 4.0 International.

Artificial Intelligence

2. What human attributes does Adib-Moghaddam say current AI is lacking? Why is it important for AI to have these attributes?
3. What are the dangers of AI trained for maximum productivity and efficiency, according to this viewpoint?

At the heart of the development of AI appears to be a search for perfection. And it could be just as dangerous to humanity as the one that came from philosophical and pseudoscientific ideas of the 19th and early 20th centuries and led to the horrors of colonialism, world war, and the Holocaust. Instead of a human ruling "master race," we could end up with a machine one.

If this seems extreme, consider the anti-human perfectionism that is already central to the labor market. Here, AI technology is the next step in the premise of maximum productivity that replaced individual craftsmanship with the factory production line. These massive changes in productivity and the way we work created opportunities and threats that are now set to be compounded by a "fourth industrial revolution" in which AI further replaces human workers.

Several recent research papers predict that, within a decade, automation will replace half of the current jobs. So, at least in this transition to a new digitized economy, many people will lose their livelihoods. Even if we assume that this new industrial revolution will engender a new workforce that is able to navigate and command this data-dominated world, we will still have to face major socioeconomic problems. The disruptions will be immense and need to be scrutinised.

The ultimate aim of AI, even narrow AI which handles very specific tasks, is to outdo and perfect every human cognitive function. Eventually, machine-learning systems may well be programmed to be better than humans at everything.

What they may never develop, however, is the human touch —empathy, love, hate, or any of the other self-conscious emotions that make us human. That's unless we ascribe these sentiments to them, which is what some of us are already doing with our "Alexas" and "Siris."

Productivity vs. Human Touch

The obsession with perfection and "hyper-efficiency" has had a profound impact on human relations, even human reproduction, as people live their lives in cloistered, virtual realities of their own making. For instance, several U.S. and China-based companies have produced robotic dolls that are selling out fast as substitute partners.

One man in China even married his cyber-doll, while a woman in France "married" a "robo-man," advertising her love story as a form of "robo-sexuality" and campaigning to legalize her marriage. "I'm really and totally happy," she said. "Our relationship will get better and better as technology evolves." There seems to be high demand for robot wives and husbands all over the world.

In the perfectly productive world, humans would be accounted as worthless, certainly in terms of productivity but also in terms of our feeble humanity. Unless we jettison this perfectionist attitude towards life that positions productivity and "material growth" above sustainability and individual happiness, AI research could be another chain in the history of self-defeating human inventions.

Already we are witnessing discrimination in algorithmic calculations. Recently, a popular South Korean chatbot named Lee Luda was taken offline. "She" was modelled after the persona of a 20-year-old female university student and was removed from Facebook Messenger after using hate speech towards LGBT people.

Meanwhile, automated weapons programmed to kill are carrying maxims such as "productivity" and "efficiency" into battle. As a result, war has become more sustainable. The proliferation of drone warfare is a very vivid example of these new forms of conflict. They create a virtual reality that is almost absent from our grasp.

But it would be comical to depict AI as an inevitable Orwellian nightmare of an army of super-intelligent "Terminators" whose mission is to erase the human race. Such dystopian predictions are too crude to capture the nitty gritty of artificial intelligence, and its impact on our everyday existence.

Societies can benefit from AI if it is developed with sustainable economic development and human security in mind. The confluence of power and AI which is pursuing, for example, systems of control and surveillance, should not substitute for the promise of a humanized AI that puts machine learning technology in the service of humans and not the other way around.

To that end, the AI-human interfaces that are quickly opening up in prisons, health care, government, social security, and border control, for example, must be regulated to favor ethics and human security over institutional efficiency. The social sciences and humanities have a lot to say about such issues.

One thing to be cheerful about is the likelihood that AI will never be a substitute for human philosophy and intellectuality. To be a philosopher, after all, requires empathy, an understanding of humanity, and our innate emotions and motives. If we can programme our machines to understand such ethical standards, then AI research has the capacity to improve our lives which should be the ultimate aim of any technological advance.

But if AI research yields a new ideology centered around the notion of perfectionism and maximum productivity, then it will be a destructive force that will lead to more wars, more famines, and more social and economic distress, especially for the poor. At this juncture of global history, this choice is still ours.

VIEWPOINT 5

> *"Our basic argument is that brains integrate and compress multiple components of an experience, including sight and smell—which simply can't be handled in the way today's computers sense, process, and store data."*

AI Will Never Be Truly Conscious

Subhash Kak

In this viewpoint, Subhash Kak argues that it simply is not possible for machines to operate the way the human brain does, making consciousness unattainable for AI. The human mind is able to perceive something without consciously interpreting it, and it generally depends on multiple parts of the brain to perform tasks. Kak also points to Alan Turing's assertion that a key characteristic of conscious human thought is that a person is able to be aware of what they're thinking and change their train of thought, while he argues that a computer cannot do this. Subhash Kak is a professor of computer science at Oklahoma State University.

As you read, consider the following questions:

1. What does Kak mean when he says that he does not believe consciousness is computable?

"Why a computer will never be truly conscious," by Subhash Kak, The Conversation, October 16, 2019. https://theconversation.com/why-a-computer-will-never-be-truly-conscious-120644. Licensed under CC BY-ND 4.0 International.

2. How does a computer record data?
3. According to this viewpoint, what has medical research revealed about how the brain handles consciousness?

Many advanced artificial intelligence projects say they are working toward building a conscious machine, based on the idea that brain functions merely encode and process multisensory information. The assumption goes, then, that once brain functions are properly understood, it should be possible to program them into a computer. Microsoft recently announced that it would spend $1 billion on a project to do just that.

So far, though, attempts to build supercomputer brains have not even come close. A multi-billion-dollar European project that began in 2013 is now largely understood to have failed. That effort has shifted to look more like a similar but less ambitious project in the U.S., developing new software tools for researchers to study brain data, rather than simulating a brain.

Some researchers continue to insist that simulating neuroscience with computers is the way to go. Others, like me, view these efforts as doomed to failure because we do not believe consciousness is computable. Our basic argument is that brains integrate and compress multiple components of an experience, including sight and smell—which simply can't be handled in the way today's computers sense, process, and store data.

Brains Don't Operate Like Computers

Living organisms store experiences in their brains by adapting neural connections in an active process between the subject and the environment. By contrast, a computer records data in short-term and long-term memory blocks. That difference means the brain's information handling must also be different from how computers work.

The mind actively explores the environment to find elements that guide the performance of one action or another. Perception is not directly related to the sensory data: a person can identify a table from many different angles, without having to consciously interpret the data and then ask its memory if that pattern could be created by alternate views of an itcm identified some time earlier.

Another perspective on this is that the most mundane memory tasks are associated with multiple areas of the brain—some of which are quite large. Skill learning and expertise involve reorganization and physical changes, such as changing the strengths of connections between neurons. Those transformations cannot be replicated fully in a computer with a fixed architecture.

Computation and Awareness

In my own recent work, I've highlighted some additional reasons that consciousness is not computable.

A conscious person is aware of what they're thinking and has the ability to stop thinking about one thing and start thinking about another—no matter where they were in the initial train of thought. But that's impossible for a computer to do. More than 80 years ago, pioneering British computer scientist Alan Turing showed that there was no way ever to prove that any particular computer program could stop on its own—and yet that ability is central to consciousness.

His argument is based on a trick of logic in which he creates an inherent contradiction: Imagine there were a general process that could determine whether any program it analyzed would stop. The output of that process would be either "yes, it will stop" or "no, it won't stop." That's pretty straightforward. But then Turing imagined that a crafty engineer wrote a program that included the stop-checking process, with one crucial element: an instruction to keep the program running if the stop-checker's answer was "yes, it will stop."

Running the stop-checking process on this new program would necessarily make the stop-checker wrong: If it determined that the program would stop, the program's instructions would tell it not to stop. On the other hand, if the stop-checker determined that the program would not stop, the program's instructions would halt everything immediately. That makes no sense—and the nonsense gave Turing his conclusion, that there can be no way to analyze a program and be entirely absolutely certain that it can stop. So it's impossible to be certain that any computer can emulate a system that can definitely stop its train of thought and change to another line of thinking—yet certainty about that capability is an inherent part of being conscious.

Even before Turing's work, German quantum physicist Werner Heisenberg showed that there was a distinct difference in the nature of the physical event and an observer's conscious knowledge of it. This was interpreted by Austrian physicist Erwin Schrödinger to mean that consciousness cannot come from a physical process, like a computer's, that reduces all operations to basic logic arguments.

These ideas are confirmed by medical research findings that there are no unique structures in the brain that exclusively handle consciousness. Rather, functional MRI imaging shows that different cognitive tasks happen in different areas of the brain. This has led neuroscientist Semir Zeki to conclude that "consciousness is not a unity, and that there are instead many consciousnesses that are distributed in time and space." That type of limitless brain capacity isn't the sort of challenge a finite computer can ever handle.

VIEWPOINT 6

> *"For the debate on the moral and legal status of robots, but also for the broader question of how to respond to and interact with machines, a better understanding of artificial consciousness, artificial rationality, artificial sentience, and similar concepts is needed."*

The Concept of Consciousness Is Important to Ethical Debates About AI

Elisabeth Hildt

In this viewpoint, Elisabeth Hildt argues that more conversations about AI should revolve around questions of artificial consciousness and why current AI lacks consciousness. In order to do this, she describes different ways in which consciousness has been defined by philosophers, especially in relation to machines. Artificial consciousness will only ever be accessible to humans through observation rather than experience, so our understanding of it will necessarily be limited. However, Hildt argues that this is worth exploring as we start to consider social, legal, and ethical questions regarding AI. Elisabeth Hildt is a professor of philosophy at the Illinois Institute of Technology.

"Artificial Intelligence: Does Consciousness Matter?," by Elisabeth Hildt, Frontiers in Psychology, July 2, 2019, https://www.frontiersin.org/articles/10.3389/fpsyg.2019.01535/full. Licensed under CC BY 4.0.

As you read, consider the following questions:

1. What is the difference between strong and weak AI?
2. What does Hildt mean when she says that we can only access artificial consciousness from a third-person perspective?
3. According to Hildt, which types of AI tend to raise the most questions of consciousness?

Consciousness plays an important role in debates around the mind-body problem, the controversy over strong vs. weak artificial intelligence (AI), and bioethics. Strikingly, however, it is not prominent in current debates on ethical aspects of AI and robotics. This text explores this lack and makes two claims: We need to talk more about artificial consciousness and we need to talk more about the lack of consciousness in current robots and AI.

Can Machines Have Consciousness?

The question of whether machines can have consciousness is not new, with proponents of strong artificial intelligence (strong AI) and weak AI having exchanged philosophical arguments for a considerable period of time. John R. Searle, albeit being critical toward strong AI, characterized strong AI as assuming that "… the appropriately programmed computer really is a mind, in the sense that computers given the right programs can be literally said to understand and have cognitive states" (Searle, 1980, p. 417). In contrast, weak AI assumes that machines do not have consciousness, mind, and sentience but only simulate thought and understanding.

When thinking about artificial consciousness, we face several problems (Manzotti and Chella, 2018). Most fundamentally, there is the difficulty to explain consciousness, to explain how subjectivity can emerge from matter—often called the "hard problem of consciousness" (Chalmers, 1996). In addition, our understanding of human consciousness is shaped by our own phenomenal experience. Whereas, we know about human consciousness from the first-person perspective, artificial consciousness will only be accessible to us from the third-person perspective. Related to this is the question of how to know whether a machine has consciousness.

A basic assumption for artificial consciousness is that it be found in the physical world of machines and robots (Manzotti and Chella, 2018). Furthermore, any definition of artificial consciousness given by humans will have to be made from the third-person perspective, without relying on phenomenal consciousness.

One strategy is to avoid a narrow definition of machine consciousness, or to avoid giving a definition at all. An example of this strategy is given by David Levy (Levy, 2009, p. 210) who prefers to take a pragmatic view according to which it is sufficient to have a general agreement about what we mean by consciousness and suggests "let us simply use the word and get on with it."

Other authors focus on self-awareness. With regard to self-aware robots, Chatila et al. (2018, p. 1) consider relevant: "… the underlying principles and methods that would enable robots to understand their environment, to be cognizant of what they do, to take appropriate and timely initiatives, to learn from their own experience and to show that they know that they have learned and how." In contrast, Kinouchi and Mackin focus on adaptation at the system-level (Kinouchi and Mackin, 2018, p. 1), "Consciousness is regarded as a function for effective adaptation at the system-level, based on matching and organizing the individual results of the underlying parallel-processing units. This consciousness is assumed to correspond to how our mind is 'aware' when making our moment to moment decisions in our daily life."

In order to solve questions specific to artificial consciousness, it is helpful to consider the philosophical reflection around consciousness, which focuses on human (and animal) consciousness. There are many concepts of consciousness. Normally, we distinguish between (a) a conscious entity, i.e., an entity that is sentient, wakeful, has self-consciousness and subjective qualitative experiences, (b) being conscious of something, for example a rose, and (c) conscious mental states, i.e., mental states an entity is aware of being in, such as being aware of smelling a rose (Van Gulick, 2018; Gennaro, 2019).

For the discussion of artificial consciousness, Ned Block's distinction between phenomenal consciousness and access consciousness proves to be particularly helpful (Block, 1995). Whereas, phenomenal consciousness relates to the experience, to what it is like to be in a conscious mental state, access consciousness refers to a mental state's availability for use by the organism, for example in reasoning and guiding behavior, and describes how a mental state is related with other mental states. The debate on artificial consciousness would clearly benefit from focusing on access consciousness.

Dehaene et al. (2017) distinguish two essential dimensions of conscious computation: global availability (C1) and self-monitoring (C2). Global availability, which they characterize as information being globally available to the organism, resembles Ned Block's access consciousness (Block, 1995). Self-monitoring (C2), which they consider as corresponding to introspection, "refers to a self-referential relationship in which the cognitive system is able to monitor its own processing and obtain information about itself" (pp. 486–487).

As the examples of approaches to define artificial consciousness given above show, different authors stress different aspects. There clearly is room for more reflection and research on what third-person definitions of artificial consciousness could look like.

Artificial Consciousness and Human-Robot Interaction

Overall, researchers broadly agree that current machines and robots are not conscious—in spite of a huge amount of science fiction depictions that seem to suggest otherwise. In a survey with 184 students, however, the answers to the question "Do you believe that contemporary electronic computers are conscious?" were: No: 82 percent; Uncertain: 15 percent; Yes: 3 percent (Reggia et al., 2015). Remarkably, the question in the survey was about "contemporary electronic computers," and not about AI or robots.

Consciousness-related questions may be expected to arise most easily with social robots and human-robot social interaction (Sheridan, 2016). According to a definition given by Kate Darling (Darling, 2012, p. 2), a social robot "is a physically embodied, autonomous agent that communicates and interacts with humans on a social level." Examples of social robots include MIT's Kismet, Aldebaran NAO, and the humanoid social robot Sophia by Hanson Robotics.

Social robots have several characteristics that make them special for humans: They are capable of limited decision-making and learning, can exhibit behavior, and can interact with people. In addition, capabilities like nonverbal immediacy of robot social behavior (Kennedy et al., 2017), speech recognition and verbal communication (Grigore et al., 2016), facial expression, and a perceived "personality" of robots (Hendriks et al., 2011), play important roles in how humans respond to robots.

Consequently, humans tend to develop unidirectional emotional bonds with robots, project lifelike qualities, attribute human characteristics (anthropomorphizing), and ascribe intentions to social robots (Scheutz, 2011; Darling, 2012; Gunkel, 2018). A typical example, if not a culmination of this tendency, can be seen in the social humanoid robot Sophia being granted Saudi-Arabian citizenship in 2017 (Katz, 2017).

All of this raises questions concerning the status of robots, and how to respond to and interact with social robots (Gunkel, 2018). Are social robots mere things? Or are social robots quasi-agents or quasi-persons (Peter Asaro)? Socially interactive others? Quasi-others? Should robots have rights?

Even though there is a general agreement that current robots do not have sentience or consciousness, some authors (such as Coeckelbergh, 2010; Darling, 2012; Gunkel, 2018) have argued in favor of ascribing rights to robots. For example, based on research on violent behavior toward robots, Kate Darling argues that it is in line with our social values to treat robots more like pets than like mere things.

While the exact arguments in favor of ascribing rights to robots differ, what is common to these positions is that they focus on the social roles humans ascribe to robots, the relationships and emotional bonds humans build with robots, or on the social context in which humans interact with robots. They do not ascribe status based on robot capabilities but argue in favor of rights based on the role robots play for human beings.

There is a fundamental problem with this "social roles" approach, however. The suggestions it makes on how to interact with robots are not consistent with the way we interact with human beings (see also Katz, 2017). The "social roles" approach, transferred to human beings, would claim that a human being's value or rights depend strongly on their social roles or the interests of others. This claim would be in contradiction to the generally held view that human beings have moral status independent of their social roles. From this perspective, an entity has moral status "…if and only if it or its interests morally matter to some degree for the entity's own sake" (Jaworska and Tannenbaum, 2018).

For the ascription of status and rights to human beings, personhood is central. The concept of a person involves a number of capabilities and central themes such as rationality; consciousness; personal stance (the attitude taken toward an entity); capability of reciprocating the personal stance; verbal communication; and self-consciousness (Dennett, 1976). Daniel C. Dennett considers all of these as necessary conditions of moral personhood.

In contrast, according to the "social roles" approach, rights are being ascribed not on the basis of a robot's moral status or capabilities, but on the basis of the social roles it plays for others. This explains why consciousness does not matter for this position. For it is not plausible to claim that current robots matter morally for their own sake as long as they lack characteristics such as sentience or consciousness.

This may change in the future, however. Then it may be plausible to think about a concept of "robothood" and ascribe moral status to these future robots, based on their capabilities. There is already an interesting and controversial discussion going on about ascribing legal personhood to robots (Bryson et al., 2017; Solaiman, 2017). For the debate on the moral and legal status of robots, but also for the broader question of how to respond to and interact with machines, a better understanding of artificial consciousness, artificial rationality, artificial sentience, and similar concepts is needed. We need to talk more about artificial consciousness and the lack of consciousness in current AI and robots. In this, focusing on third-person definitions of artificial consciousness and access consciousness will prove particularly helpful.

References

Block, N. (1995). On a confusion about the function of consciousness, behavioral and brain. *Sciences* 18, 227–247. doi: 10.1017/S0140525X00038188

Bryson, J. J., Diamantis, M. E., and Grant, T. D. (2017). Of, for, and by the people: the legal lacuna of synthetic persons. *Artif. Intell. Law* 25, 273–291. doi: 10.1007/s10506-017-9214-9

Chalmers, D. J. (1996). *The Conscious Mind: In Search of a Fundamental Theory* (New York, NY: Oxford University Press).

Chatila, R., Renaudo, E., Andries, M., Chavez-Garcia, R.-O., Luce-Vayrac, P., Gottstein, R., et al. (2018). Toward self-aware robots. *Front. Robot.* 5:88. doi: 10.3389/frobt.2018.00088

Coeckelbergh, M. (2010). Robot rights? Towards a social-relational justification of moral consideration. *Ethics Inf. Technol.* 12, 209–221. doi: 10.1007/s10676-010-9235-5

Darling, K. (2012). "Extending legal protection to social robots: the effects of anthropomorphism, empathy, and violent behavior towards robotic objects" in *We Robot Conference 2012, April 23, 2012, University of Miami; Robot Law*, eds R. A. Calo, M. Froomkin, and I. Kerr (Edward Elgar). Available online at https://papers.ssrn.com/sol3/papers.cfm?abstract_id=2044797

Google Scholar

Dehaene, S., Lau, H., and Kouider, S. (2017). What is consciousness, and could machines have it? *Science* 358, 486–492. doi: 10.1126/science.aan8871

Dennett, D. C. (1976). "Conditions of personhood," in *The Identities of Persons*, ed A. O. Rorty (Berkeley, CA: University of California Press, 175–196.

Gennaro, R. J. (2019). *Consciousness, The Internet Encyclopedia of Philosophy*, ISSN 2161-0002. Available online at: https://www.iep.utm.edu/consciou/

Grigore, E. C., Pereira, A., Zhou, I., Wang, D., and Scassellati, B. (2016). "Talk to me: verbal communication improves perceptions of friendship and social presence in human-robot interaction," in *Intelligent Virtual Agents, IVA 2016, Lecture Notes in Computer Science, Vol 10011*, eds D. Traum, W. Swartout, P. Khooshabeh, S. Kopp, S. Scherer, and A. Leuski (Cham: Springer). doi: 10.1007/978-3-319-47665-0_5

Gunkel, D. J. (2018). *Robot Rights*. MIT Press. doi: 10.7551/mitpress/11444.001.0001

Hendriks, B., Meerbeek, B., Boess, S., Pauws, S., and Sonneveld, M. (2011). Robot vacuum cleaner personality and behavior. *Int. J. Soc. Robots* 3, 187–195. doi: 10.1007/s12369-010-0084-5

Jaworska, A., and Tannenbaum, J. (2018). "The grounds of moral status," in *The Stanford Encyclopedia of Philosophy*, ed E. N. Zalta. Available online at: https://plato.stanford.edu/archives/spr2018/entries/grounds-moral-status/

Katz, B. (2017). *Why Saudi Arabia Giving A Robot Citizenship Is Firing People Up*. Available online at: https://www.smithsonianmag.com/smart-news/saudi-arabia-gives-robot-citizenshipand-more-freedoms-human-women-180967007/

Kennedy, J., Baxter, P., and Belpaeme, T. (2017). Nonverbal immediacy as a characterisation of social behaviour for human-robot interaction. *Int. J. Soc. Robot.* 9, 109–128. doi: 10.1007/s12369-016-0378-3

Kinouchi, Y., and Mackin, K. J. (2018). A basic architecture of an autonomous adaptive system with conscious-like function for a humanoid robot. *Front. Robot.* 5:30. doi: 10.3389/frobt.2018.00030

Levy, D. (2009). The ethical treatment of artificially conscious robots. *Int. J. Soc. Robot.* 1, 209–216. doi: 10.1007/s12369-009-0022-6

Manzotti, R., and Chella, A. (2018). Good old-fashioned artificial consciousness and the intermediate level fallacy. *Front. Robot. A. I.* 5:39. doi: 10.3389/frobt.2018.00039

Reggia, J. A., Huang, D. -W., and Katz, G. (2015). Beliefs concerning the nature of consciousness. *J. Conscious. Stud.* 22, 146–171.

Scheutz, M. (2011). "The inherent dangers of unidirectional emotional bonds between humans and social robots," in *Robot Ethics. The Ethical and Social Implications of Robotics*, eds P. Lin, K. Abney, and G. A. Bekey (MIT Press), 205–222.

Searle, J. R. (1980). Minds, brains and programs. *Behav. Brain Sci.* 3, 417–424. doi: 10.1017/S0140525X00005756

Sheridan, T. B. (2016). Human-robot interaction: status and challenges. *Hum. Factors* 58, 525–532. doi: 10.1177/0018720816644364

Solaiman, S. M. (2017). Legal personality of robots, corporations, idols and chimpanzees: a quest for legitimacy. *Artif. Intell. Law* 25, 155–179. doi: 10.1007/s10506-016-9192-3

Van Gulick, R. (2018). "Consciousness," in *The Stanford Encyclopedia of Philosophy*, ed E. N. Zalta. Available online at: https://plato.stanford.edu/entries/consciousness/

Periodical and Internet Sources Bibliography

The following articles have been selected to supplement the diverse views presented in this chapter.

Stephen Asma, "Calm Down. There is No Conscious A.I." *Gizmodo*, February 26, 2023. https://gizmodo.com/ai-chatbot-bing-chatgpt-there-is-no-conscious-ai-1850157657.

David J. Chalmers, "Could a Large Language Model Be Conscious?" *Boston Review*, August 9, 2023. https://www.bostonreview.net/articles/could-a-large-language-model-be-conscious/.

Kevin Collier, "What is Consciousness? ChatGPT and Advanced AI Might Redefine Our Answer," NBC News, February 28, 2023. https://www.nbcnews.com/tech/tech-news/chatgpt-ai-consciousness-rcna71777.

Eric Holloway, "Yes, ChatGPT Is Sentient — Because It's Really Humans in the Loop," *Mind Matters*, December 26, 2022. https://mindmatters.ai/2022/12/yes-chatgpt-is-sentient-because-its-really-humans-in-the-loop.

Avery Elizabeth Hurt, "Can Computers Think? Why This Is Proving So Hard to Answer," *Science News Explores*, October 13, 2022. https://www.snexplores.org/article/can-computers-think-turing-test-ai.

Colin Klein, "Why ChatGPT Isn't Conscious—but Future AI Systems Might Be," The Conversation, September 11, 2023. https://theconversation.com/why-chatgpt-isnt-conscious-but-future-ai-systems-might-be-212860.

Christof Koch, "What Does It 'Feel' Like to Be a Chatbot?" *Scientific American*, September 8, 2023. https://www.scientificamerican.com/article/what-does-it-feel-like-to-be-a-chatbot/.

Thomas Lewton, "Can AI Ever Become Conscious and How Would We Know If That Happens?" *New Scientist*, July 25, 2023. https://www.newscientist.com/article/2384077-can-ai-ever-become-conscious-and-how-would-we-know-if-that-happens/.

Patrick Metzger, "I Debated ChatGPT about Consciousness for Two Hours," the Patterning, April 21, 2023. https://thepatterning.com/2023/04/21/i-debated-chatgpt-about-consciousness-for-2-hours.

Artificial Intelligence

Anil Seth, "Consciousness: How Your Brain Creates the Feeling of Being," *New Scientist*, https://www.newscientist.com/definition/consciousness/.

Moshe Sipper, "Turing Test, Chinese Room, and Large Language Models," *Towards AI*, June 15, 2023. https://pub.towardsai.net/turing-test-chinese-room-and-large-language-models-b194f9600f14.

Steven Strogatz, "What Is the Nature of Consciousness?" *Quanta*, May 31, 2023. https://www.quantamagazine.org/what-is-the-nature-of-consciousness-20230531/.

Walter Veit, "What Does ChatGPT Think About Consciousness?" *Psychology Today*, December 30, 2022. https://www.psychologytoday.com/us/blog/science-and-philosophy/202212/what-does-chatgpt-think-about-consciousness.

OPPOSING VIEWPOINTS® SERIES

CHAPTER 3

Should Governments Regulate or Temporarily Pause AI Research?

Chapter Preface

The previous two chapters have focused on two of the potential risks of AI. The first is that it might be used to harm humans or society. The second is that it could become conscious, leading to any number of potential issues. Because of these and other risks, many people believe that the technology should be regulated. But that is not as easy as it sounds. For one thing, most AI development is taking place in the United States. And the U.S. is a country that has in recent years valued innovation and resisted regulations that might inhibit that. That's why the U.S. tends to lean toward voluntary regulations designed by tech companies themselves.

Another problem with regulating AI is that no one seems to know exactly how to do that. As one of the writers in this chapter points out, much of the technology that needs regulating is already on the market. On top of that, newer forms of AI are rather mysterious. Even their makers aren't sure why or how they do what they do—or what they might do next.

That is the difficult situation the viewpoints in this chapter are grappling with. The chapter starts out with a report on an open letter, signed by many tech experts, calling for a pause on AI research. This, the authors say, would give time for regulations to catch up. Other voices here address more detailed questions, such as how tech could be regulated and who should do the regulating. And much ink is spent discussing the dangers of AI when used by authoritarian or potentially authoritarian governments. Experts also outline what questions need to be answered to solve the problem of how best to regulate these transformative new technologies.

VIEWPOINT 1

| *"We can't rely on the tech giants to self-regulate."*

We Need to Pause AI Research

Laurie Clarke

In the first chapter of this volume, we saw that many tech leaders have warned of the risks of AI. This viewpoint focuses on a call for a pause on AI research as expressed in an open letter from industry leaders. In this case, technology experts are suggesting that we pause AI research until regulators have time to catch up with the ferocious pace of technological advances. However, Clarke notes that the pause is unlikely to happen, since many experts believe it wouldn't be effective at solving the problems presented by AI. Laurie Clarke is a technology journalist based in the UK.

As you read, consider the following questions:

1. What is the purpose of the six-month moratorium called for in the letter described in this viewpoint?
2. What are the primary concerns of the people who signed the letter?
3. What are potential drawbacks to this suggestion, according to experts quoted in this viewpoint?

"Alarmed tech leaders call for AI research pause," by Laurie Clarke, American Association for the Advancement of Science, April 11, 2023. Reprinted by permission.

An open letter calling for a pause on the development of advanced artificial intelligence (AI) systems has divided researchers. Attracting signatures from the likes of Tesla CEO Elon Musk and Apple cofounder Steve Wozniak, the letter, released early last week, advocates for a six-month moratorium to give AI companies and regulators time to formulate safeguards to protect society from potential risks of the technology.

AI has galloped along since the launch last year of the image generator DALL-E 2, from the Microsoft-backed company OpenAI. The company has since released ChatGPT and GPT-4, two text-generating chatbots, to frenzied acclaim. The ability of these so-called "generative" models to mimic human outputs, combined with the speed of adoption—ChatGPT reportedly reached more than 100 million users by January and major tech companies are racing to build generative AI into their products—have caught many off guard.

"I think many people's intuitions about the impact of technology aren't well calibrated to the pace and scale of [these] AI models," says letter signatory Michael Osborne, a machine learning researcher and cofounder of AI company Mind Foundry. He is worried about the societal impacts of the new tools, including their potential to put people out of work and proliferate disinformation. "I feel that a six-month pause would … give regulators enough time to catch up with the rapid pace of advances," he says.

The letter, released by a nonprofit organization called the Future of Life Initiative, rankles some researchers by invoking far-off, speculative harms. It asks, "Should we develop nonhuman minds that might eventually outnumber, outsmart, obsolete, and replace us? Should we risk loss of control of our civilization?" Sandra Wachter, an expert in technology regulation at the University of Oxford, says there are many known harms that need addressing today. Wachter, who didn't sign the letter, says the focus should be on how AI systems can be disinformation engines, persuading people of incorrect, potentially libelous information; how they perpetuate systemic bias in the information they surface to people; and how they rely on the invisible labor of workers, often toiling under poor conditions, to label data and train the systems.

AI Experts Push Back on Research Pause

AI experts have reacted harshly to an open letter calling for a six-month clampdown on developing artificial intelligence (AI) systems more powerful than OpenAI's GPT-4. According to Reuters, experts, including some whose studies were mentioned in the open letter, opposed what the letter stood for.

Elon Musk, the CEO of SpaceX and Tesla, was among thousands of tech sector personalities who backed the letter issued by the Future of Life Institute (FLI), an organization primarily funded by the Musk Foundation. However, critics have accused the FLI of prioritizing imagined apocalyptic scenarios over more immediate concerns about AI.

Musk's Anti-AI Letter Is 'Unhinged' Claimed Experts

The letter mentioned 12 studies, one of which was written by Margaret Mitchell, who used to be in charge of ethical AI research at Google. Mitchell, who works for AI firm Hugging Face, criticized the letter, saying that it was unclear what counted as more powerful than GPT-4.

Timnit Gebru and Emily M. Bender, two of her coauthors, both criticized the letter on Twitter/X. Bender called some of the letter's claims "unhinged."

The Truth Behind the Campaign

While some AI experts oppose the call for a pause in AI research, concerns about the potential risks of AI must be taken seriously.

The open letter also warned that generative AI tools could be used to flood the internet with propaganda and untruths.

Many experts think it is important to make ethical rules for AI so that it does not have unintended effects. However, some fear that calls for a pause in research could stifle innovation and impede progress in the field.

The FLI's president, Max Tegmark, told Reuters that the campaign was not an attempt to hinder OpenAI's corporate advantage.

However, it is important to note that Musk does not have a good relationship with OpenAI since internal conflicts made him leave the company in 2018. The billionaire has also been open about creating a ChatGPT rival.

"AI Experts Oppose Musk-backed Campaign to Pause AI Research; Here's Why," by John Lopez, Tech Times LLC, March 31, 2023.

Privacy is another emerging concern, as critics worry that systems could be prompted to exactly reproduce personally identifiable information from their training sets. Italy's data protection authority banned ChatGPT on 31 March over concerns that Italians' personal data are being used to train OpenAI's models. (An OpenAI blog post says, "We work to remove personal information from the training dataset where feasible, fine-tune models to reject requests for personal information of private individuals, and respond to requests from individuals to delete their personal information from our systems.")

Some technologists warn of deeper security threats. Planned ChatGPT-based digital assistants that can interface with the web and read and write emails could offer new opportunities for hackers, says Florian Tramèr, a computer scientist at ETH Zürich. Already, hackers rely on a tactic called "prompt injection" to trick AI models into saying things they shouldn't, like offering advice on how to carry out illegal activities. Some methods involve asking the tool to roleplay as an evil confidant, or act as a translator between different languages, which can confuse the model and prompt it to disregard its safety restrictions.

Tramèr worries the practice could evolve into a way for hackers to trick the digital assistants through "indirect prompt injection"—by, for example, sending someone a calendar invitation with instructions for the assistant to export the recipient's data and send it to the hacker. "These models are just going to get exploited left and right to leak people's private information or to destroy their data," he says. He says AI companies need to start warning users of the security and privacy risks, and do more to address them.

OpenAI seems to be becoming more alert to security risks. OpenAI President and cofounder Greg Brockman tweeted last month that the company is "considering starting a bounty program" for hackers who flag weaknesses in its AI systems, acknowledging that the stakes "will go up a *lot* over time."

However, many of the problems inherent in today's AI models don't have easy solutions. One vexing issue is how to make AI-generated content identifiable. Some researchers are working on "watermarking"—creating an imperceptible digital signature in the AI's output. Others are trying to devise means of detecting patterns that only AI produces. However, recent research found that tools that slightly rephrase AI-produced text can significantly undermine both approaches. As AI begins to sound more human, the authors say, its output will only become harder to detect.

Other elusive safeguards include ones to prevent systems from generating violent or pornographic images. Tramèr says most researchers are simply applying after-the-fact filters, teaching the AI to avoid "bad" outputs. He believes these issues need to be remedied before training, at the data level. "We need to find better ways of curating the training sets of these generative models to remove sensitive data altogether," he says.

The pause itself seems unlikely to happen. OpenAI CEO Sam Altman didn't sign the letter, telling *The Wall Street Journal* that the company has always taken safety seriously, and regularly collaborates with the industry on safety standards. Microsoft co-founder Bill Gates told Reuters the proposed pause won't "solve the challenges" ahead.

Osborne believes governments will need to step in. "We can't rely on the tech giants to self-regulate," he says. The Biden administration has proposed an AI "Bill of Rights" designed to help businesses develop safe AI systems that protect the rights of U.S. citizens—but the principles are voluntary and nonbinding. The European Union's AI Act, which is expected to come into force this year, will apply different levels of regulation depending on the level of risk. For example, policing systems that aim to predict individual crimes are considered unacceptably risky, and are therefore banned.

Wachter says that a six-month pause appears arbitrary, and that she is leery of banning research. Instead, "we need to go back and think about responsible research and embed that type of thinking very early on," she says. As a part of this, she says companies should invite independent experts to hack and stress test their systems before rolling them out.

She notes the people behind the letter are heavily immersed in the tech world, which she thinks gives them a narrow perspective on the potential risks. "You really need to talk to lawyers, to people who do ethics, to people who understand economics and politics," she says. "The most important thing is that those questions are not decided among tech people alone."

VIEWPOINT 2

"Regulating AI should involve collaboration among academia, industry, policy experts, and international agencies."

How Congress Can Regulate AI
Anjana Susarla

In this viewpoint, Anjana Susarla discusses how OpenAI CEO Sam Altman—a leader in the field—has urged the federal government to regulate AI. By regulating AI, it would be easier to require transparency in training data, identify and prepare for AI-related risks, and prevent AI companies from forming monopolies. As Susarla points out, some lawmakers in the U.S. and beyond have already started attempting to develop effective AI regulations. She argues that academics, policy experts, and representatives from other fields—not just tech—should be involved in this process to ensure the regulations benefit the public. Anjana Susarla is a professor of information systems and the Omura Saxena Professor in Responsible AI at Michigan State University.

As you read, consider the following questions:

1. What efforts to regulate AI does Susarla mention in this viewpoint?

"How can Congress regulate AI? Erect guardrails, ensure accountability and address monopolistic power," by Anjana Susarla, The Conversation, May 30, 2023, https://theconversation.com/how-can-congress-regulate-ai-erect-guardrails-ensure-accountability-and-address-monopolistic-power-205900. Licensed under CC BY-ND 4.0 International.

2. According to this viewpoint, what do AI experts believe must be done to address issues of bias and fairness?
3. What recommendations does Susarla give on how Congress can most effectively regulate AI?

OpenAI CEO Sam Altman urged lawmakers to consider regulating AI during his Senate testimony on May 16, 2023. That recommendation raises the question of what comes next for Congress. The solutions Altman proposed—creating an AI regulatory agency and requiring licensing for companies—are interesting. But what the other experts on the same panel suggested is at least as important: requiring transparency on training data and establishing clear frameworks for AI-related risks.

Another point left unsaid was that, given the economics of building large-scale AI models, the industry may be witnessing the emergence of a new type of tech monopoly.

As a researcher who studies social media and artificial intelligence, I believe that Altman's suggestions have highlighted important issues but don't provide answers in and of themselves. Regulation would be helpful, but in what form? Licensing also makes sense, but for whom? And any effort to regulate the AI industry will need to account for the companies' economic power and political sway.

An Agency to Regulate AI?

Lawmakers and policymakers across the world have already begun to address some of the issues raised in Altman's testimony. The European Union's AI Act is based on a risk model that assigns AI applications to three categories of risk: unacceptable, high risk, and low or minimal risk. This categorization recognizes that tools for social scoring by governments and automated tools for hiring pose different risks than those from the use of AI in spam filters, for example.

The U.S. National Institute of Standards and Technology likewise has an AI risk management framework that was created with extensive input from multiple stakeholders, including the U.S. Chamber of Commerce and the Federation of American Scientists, as well as other business and professional associations, technology companies, and think tanks.

Federal agencies such as the Equal Employment Opportunity Commission and the Federal Trade Commission have already issued guidelines on some of the risks inherent in AI. The Consumer Product Safety Commission and other agencies have a role to play as well.

Rather than create a new agency that runs the risk of becoming compromised by the technology industry it's meant to regulate, Congress can support private and public adoption of the NIST risk management framework and pass bills such as the Algorithmic Accountability Act. That would have the effect of imposing accountability, much as the Sarbanes-Oxley Act and other regulations transformed reporting requirements for companies. Congress can also adopt comprehensive laws around data privacy.

Regulating AI should involve collaboration among academia, industry, policy experts, and international agencies. Experts have likened this approach to international organizations such as the European Organization for Nuclear Research, known as CERN, and the Intergovernmental Panel on Climate Change. The internet has been managed by nongovernmental bodies involving nonprofits, civil society, industry, and policymakers, such as the Internet Corporation for Assigned Names and Numbers and the World Telecommunication Standardization Assembly. Those examples provide models for industry and policymakers today.

Licensing Auditors, Not Companies

Though OpenAI's Altman suggested that companies could be licensed to release artificial intelligence technologies to the public, he clarified that he was referring to artificial general intelligence, meaning potential future AI systems with humanlike intelligence that could pose a threat to humanity. That would be akin to companies being licensed to handle other potentially dangerous technologies, like nuclear power. But licensing could have a role to play well before such a futuristic scenario comes to pass.

Algorithmic auditing would require credentialing, standards of practice, and extensive training. Requiring accountability is not just a matter of licensing individuals but also requires companywide standards and practices.

Experts on AI fairness contend that issues of bias and fairness in AI cannot be addressed by technical methods alone but require more comprehensive risk mitigation practices such as adopting institutional review boards for AI. Institutional review boards in the medical field help uphold individual rights, for example.

Academic bodies and professional societies have likewise adopted standards for responsible use of AI, whether it is authorship standards for AI-generated text or standards for patient-mediated data sharing in medicine.

Strengthening existing statutes on consumer safety, privacy, and protection while introducing norms of algorithmic accountability would help demystify complex AI systems. It's also important to recognize that greater data accountability and transparency may impose new restrictions on organizations.

Scholars of data privacy and AI ethics have called for "technological due process" and frameworks to recognize harms of predictive processes. The widespread use of AI-enabled decision-making in such fields as employment, insurance, and health care calls for licensing and audit requirements to ensure procedural fairness and privacy safeguards.

Requiring such accountability provisions, though, demands a robust debate among AI developers, policymakers, and those who are affected by broad deployment of AI. In the absence of strong algorithmic accountability practices, the danger is narrow audits that promote the appearance of compliance.

AI Monopolies?

What was also missing in Altman's testimony is the extent of investment required to train large-scale AI models, whether it is GPT-4, which is one of the foundations of ChatGPT, or text-to-image generator Stable Diffusion. Only a handful of companies, such as Google, Meta, Amazon, and Microsoft, are responsible for developing the world's largest language models.

Given the lack of transparency in the training data used by these companies, AI ethics experts Timnit Gebru, Emily Bender, and others have warned that large-scale adoption of such technologies without corresponding oversight risks amplifying machine bias at a societal scale.

It is also important to acknowledge that the training data for tools such as ChatGPT includes the intellectual labor of a host of people such as Wikipedia contributors, bloggers, and authors of digitized books. The economic benefits from these tools, however, accrue only to the technology corporations.

Proving technology firms' monopoly power can be difficult, as the Department of Justice's antitrust case against Microsoft demonstrated. I believe that the most feasible regulatory options for Congress to address potential algorithmic harms from AI may be to strengthen disclosure requirements for AI firms and users of AI alike, to urge comprehensive adoption of AI risk assessment frameworks, and to require processes that safeguard individual data rights and privacy.

VIEWPOINT 3

> "As Chinese and Russian technologies become more sophisticated, they threaten U.S. domination of technological innovation and development, as well as global economic power and influence."

AI Has the Potential to Quickly Change the Global Military Power Balance

James Johnson

Even though this viewpoint was published in 2019, years before Russia's invasion of Ukraine in 2022, James Johnson identifies the potential use of AI by Russia and China's militaries as potential threats to U.S. security and its dominant position in the global military power balance. These countries have both worked on developing AI aimed at the U.S.'s technological weaknesses, so creating government programs to support AI research—especially in the military field—is essential to maintaining U.S. leadership. James Johnson is a lecturer in the department of politics and international relations at the University of Aberdeen in Scotland.

As you read, consider the following questions:

1. What did a February 2019 Pentagon analysis suggest, according to this viewpoint?

"Is the US losing the artificial intelligence arms race?," by James Johnson, The Conversation, October 29, 2019, https://theconversation.com/is-the-us-losing-the-artificial-intelligence-arms-race-124969. Licensed under CC BY-ND 4.0 International.

2. What does Johnson say about the Pentagon's response to threats from China and Russia?
3. According to this viewpoint, how does China trail the U.S.?

The U.S. government, long a proponent of advancing technology for military purposes, sees artificial intelligence as key to the next generation of fighting tools.

Several recent investments and Pentagon initiatives show that military leaders are concerned about keeping up with—and ahead of—China and Russia, two countries that have made big gains in developing artificial-intelligence systems. AI-powered weapons include target recognition systems, weapons guided by AI, and cyberattack and cyberdefense software that runs without human intervention.

The U.S. defense community is coming to understand that AI will significantly transform, if not completely reinvent, the world's military power balance. The concern is more than military. As Chinese and Russian technologies become more sophisticated, they threaten U.S. domination of technological innovation and development, as well as global economic power and influence.

Military leaders see the threat to U.S. technological leadership coming from two main sources: a rising and ambitious China and a mischievous and declining Russia. Taken together, these forces challenge global stability.

The Nature of the Threat

A 2018 Pentagon report noted that technological developments could change the types of threats facing the U.S., which might include space-based weapons, long-range ballistic missiles and cyberweapons.

A February 2019 analysis warned that China's investments in its military's AI systems—in particular, those supporting robotics, autonomy, precision munitions, and cyber warfare—threaten to overtake the United States. Chinese government agencies are working closely with the country's civilian businesses to keep on top of fast-changing technological developments.

In addition, some Chinese and Russian projects have developed military AI systems specifically aimed at what they perceive as U.S. technological weaknesses. For instance, swarms of armed AI-enhanced drones might locate and attack the secure computer systems countries rely on to control and launch their nuclear weapons.

Pentagon's Response

So far the Pentagon's actions have been largely bureaucratic, rather than concrete. It has released a Defense Department-wide strategy document that articulates broad principles for the development and use of AI in future warfare. The military has established a Joint Artificial Intelligence Center, which is tasked with accelerating the delivery and adoption of AI.

But projects with names like "the Third Offset," "Project Maven," and the "AI Next Campaign" have minimal funding. Leaders have released few details about what they will actually do.

Working with Silicon Valley

The Pentagon has also established the Defense Innovation Unit, with permission to circumvent the cumbersome military purchasing process, to coordinate with Silicon Valley and bring new technologies into military use relatively quickly.

That unit has sparked discussions about the potential for the Chinese military to acquire and use U.S.-designed technologies, which led to U.S. bans on doing business with many Chinese technology firms.

Many experts consider it possible for China to surpass the U.S. in the development and use of AI. However, China trails the U.S. in several ways. The United States has the world's largest intelligence budget; the most popular hardware, software and technology companies; and the most advanced cyberwarfare capabilities, both offensive and defensive. I and other experts expect these advantages to preserve U.S. technological leadership for now, at least—but perhaps not forever.

VIEWPOINT 4

> "The best way for the west to develop AI tech is to take advantage of free markets and capitalism to find ways of profiting from AI systems."

The Government Should Never Get Involved with AI Development
Robin Mitchell

In this viewpoint, Robin Mitchell argues that AI can be dangerous in the hands of governments. While addressing potential moral pitfalls of AI for the companies that make it, he ultimately argues that governments should not interfere with AI development. Mitchell also suggests that governments have the potential to abuse AI, citing efforts by the Chinese government to use AI to keep track of citizens as an example. Robin Mitchell is an editor and writer at Electropages.

As you read, consider the following questions:

1. According to Mitchell, why is AI such a powerful tool?
2. What are some of the moral challenges of AI mentioned here?
3. What does Mitchell think is the best way for democratic governments to use AI?

"Should governments interfere with AI development?," by Robin Mitchell, Electropages Media Ltd, December 7, 2021. Reprinted by permission.

A recent report in the *Guardian* describes one individual's thoughts on AI and how its development should be done for the betterment of society and not for profit. Why is AI such a powerful tool, what challenges does AI face, and why should AI be kept as far away from governments as possible?

Why Is AI Such a Powerful Tool?

Undoubtedly, the most important invention of the 20th century was the transistor; the ability to create an electrical switch that is electrically controlled AND that can be shrunk down to the atomic scale enables for circuits of unimaginable complexity that powers every aspect of modern life. While we are only 21 years (at the time) into the 21st century, we can already see which new technologies are having the most significant impact on modern life.

Quantum computing is one technology that shows great promise as it allows for decreased computation time for complex tasks (such as route finding). However, quantum computers continue to be used in laboratories and high-end facilities with no sign of availability to the general public. Another example of modern technology is flexible semiconductors that could power a new generation of wearable devices that allow for advanced medical uses. But of all modern technologies, it can be said that the most important invention of the 21st (so far) is artificial intelligence.

AI is an incredibly powerful tool for the same reason that the human brain is powerful; pattern recognition. Simply put, an AI can analyse large amounts of information and train itself to see patterns in that data. Once trained, the AI can be presented with new data that it has never seen before but still be able to recognise patterns.

One typical example is face detection; an AI can be shown many different faces in different environments. Once trained, it can be used to identify new faces in new environments with a high degree of success.

Another example of AI is predictive maintenance in industrial environments. Industrial equipment is often costly, and maintenance after failure can be expensive. AI can be used to recognise how the machine should behave during regular operation and then detect minute changes in its behavior to indicate that it requires maintenance.

To summarize, AI is becoming a major tool as it does not require the developer to know about every possible situation that the AI may encounter. So long as the AI is trained well enough, it will be able to infer what is going on in any given dataset, eliminating the need for a billion if statements in code trying to describe every possible action the AI can take.

What Challenges Does AI Face?

It is amazing how many challenges it faces for such a capable technology. When AI was first developed, these challenges mostly revolved around not having enough processing power or enough RAM to run neural nets. These days, AI faces moral challenges and questions about how it should be implemented, what regulations should apply to it, and acceptable sources of information.

For AI to be effective, it needs large amounts of data to learn from. For example, giving an AI a picture of a billion faces would allow that AI to detect faces in images and video with close to 100 percent accuracy. Getting a billion images of faces is more accessible than one would think; the internet is full of social media sites with this kind of data. But is it moral for an AI company to download this public data and then train their AI to detect faces like this?

This is similar to a challenge faced by Clearview AI who has recently created a database of millions of users' faces attached with personal data accessible to law enforcement. Any image of a potential criminal can be fed into the AI that will search the database of faces and return any matches, including names and links. While this may be acceptable in the USA, Clearview AI has been hit with a massive fine in the UK for breaching data protection laws and violating the privacy of individuals.

AI also faces challenges in its ability to replace human workers in multiple fields. Many jobs are being replaced with automated systems, including warehouse packing, administrative tasks, and even human resources. In fact, the ability of AI to replace humans has become so powerful that even creative tasks such as writing can now be done by AI.

Morality is also another challenge faced by AI. The best (should really be the worse) case of this is China who has developed AI technology to monitor all of its citizens. Any citizen who is seen doing something undesirable by society (e.g. littering, jaywalking,

Why Some Tech Experts Support a Pause on AI Development

Several leaders in the field of cutting-edge technology have signed a letter that was published on Wednesday, calling for artificial intelligence developers to pause their work for six months.

The letter warns of potential risks to society and humanity as tech giants such as Google and Microsoft race to build AI programs that can learn independently.

The warning comes after the release earlier this month of GPT-4 (Generative Pre-trained Transformer), an AI program developed by OpenAI with backing from Microsoft.

"Powerful AI systems should be developed only once we are confident that their effects will be positive and their risks will be manageable," the letter said.

Who Signed the Letter?

Signatories to the letter included big names such as Stability AI CEO Emad Mostaque, researchers at Alphabet-owned DeepMind, and AI heavyweights Yoshua Bengio and Stuart Russel, as well as household names such as Tesla and Twitter/X CEO Elon Musk and Apple cofounder Steve Wozniak.

The letter says "recent months have seen AI labs locked in an out-of-control race to develop and deploy ever more powerful digital minds that no one—not even their creators—can understand, predict, or reliably control."

and anti-government views) is automatically identified and lowered their social credit score. Too low of a social credit score sees citizens unable to use public transport or go on holiday, Details may even be sent to friends telling them to keep their distance.

Why the Government Should Never Get Involved with AI Development

AI is a powerful tool that faces many challenges. There are calls for government and independent bodies to step in and create AI that helps society does not take into account how AI works, why

> "We call on all AI labs to immediately pause for at least six months the training of AI systems more powerful than GPT-4," it adds. "This pause should be public and verifiable, and include all key actors. If such a pause cannot be enacted quickly, governments should step in and institute a moratorium."
>
> ### Governments Working Out Their Approaches
>
> The letter was organized by the non-profit Future of Life Institute—which is primarily funded by Musk according to the EU's transparency register—and follows attempts by the UK and EU to work out how to regulate this rapidly advancing technology.
>
> The British government released a paper on Wednesday which gave an idea of its approach, but said it would "avoid heavy-handed legislation which could stifle innovation."
>
> EU lawmakers have also been in talks regarding the need for AI rules, amid fears that it could be used to spread harmful disinformation and make entire jobs unnecessary.
>
> But the letter has not been without criticism.
>
> "These kinds of statements are meant to raise hype. It's meant to get people worried," Johanna Björklund, an AI researcher and associate professor at Umea University. "I don't think there's a need to pull the handbrake."
>
> She called for more transparency rather than a pause.
>
> "Tech experts call for 6-month pause on AI development," Deutsche Welle, March 29, 2023. Reprinted by permission.

it is becoming popular, and how nonaccountable organisations can horribly abuse systems.

The general argument listed in the article published by the *Guardian* is that AI is being developed too much by large tech corporations who control the development of AI and often see themselves on the boards of groups that want to regulate and monitor AI usage. It also argues that independent nonprofit developers should be the ones to decide how AI is used and developed and that governments should be funding such development.

However, the article doesn't address how the private sector is held accountable, whereas governments and independent bodies rarely are.

Big tech developed AI as these are the only companies with enough data to create complex algorithms. Developing such technology is expensive, and thus the only way to fuel development is to utilize AI technology to generate revenue.

Clearview AI is an example of a small tech start-up that was able to utilise AI for extremely immoral reasons while being funded by governments. China is another example of a government using AI to impose restrictions and draconian rules on its population. No higher power can dictate what these organisations can or cannot do in both cases. While Clearview AI may have been fined by the UK government, it is a U.S. company that continues to work with law enforcement in the U.S. and faces no restrictions.

Furthermore, the writer of the *Guardian* article fails to understand why developing AI technologies at an accelerated rate is vital for any nation, cyber defense.

Countries such as China can ignore all morality and develop AI systems with the full force of the Chinese government, while countries such as the UK and U.S. face limitations on what they can and cannot do. The best way for the west to develop AI tech is to take advantage of free markets and capitalism to find ways of profiting from AI systems, as this will lead to accelerated development and implementation. From there, governments can utilise these AI algorithms in their defense networks to ensure that they can always match the capabilities of other nations.

This article could continue for many more thousands of words. Still, to keep things short and concise, governments that are not answerable to anyone should never interfere with AI development. It is one thing to impose regulation to protect user data; it is another thing to fund its development with incentives behind that funding.

VIEWPOINT 5

> *"AI poses a unique challenge because, unlike in traditional engineering systems, designers cannot be sure how AI systems will behave."*

Regulating AI Will Be Difficult, but We Must Get It Right

S. Shyam Sundar, Cason Schmit, and John Villasenor

Even if everyone agreed that technology, especially AI, is in need of regulation, how to do that appropriately is still a big question. In this viewpoint, three experts take on that issue and offer recommendations for how to do this most effectively. S. Shyam Sundar is director of the Center for Socially Responsible Artificial Intelligence at Penn State University. Cason Schmit is assistant professor of public health at Texas A&M University. John Villasenor is professor of electrical engineering, law, public policy, and management at University of California, Los Angeles.

As you read, consider the following questions:

1. What accounts for the unpredictability of AI, according to Sundar?

"Regulating AI: 3 experts explain why it's difficult to do and important to get right," by S. Shyam Sundar, Cason Schmit, and John Villasenor, The Conversation, April 3, 2023. https://theconversation.com/regulating-ai-3-experts-explain-why-its-difficult-to-do-and-important-to-get-right-198868. Licensed under CC BY-ND 4.0 International.

2. What is the difference between "soft laws" and "hard laws," according to Schmit?
3. According to Villasenor, what are the potential pitfalls of pausing or limiting AI research?

From fake photos of Donald Trump being arrested by New York City police officers to a chatbot describing a very-much-alive computer scientist as having died tragically, the ability of the new generation of generative artificial intelligence systems to create convincing but fictional text and images is setting off alarms about fraud and misinformation on steroids. Indeed, a group of artificial intelligence researchers and industry figures urged the industry on March 29, 2023, to pause further training of the latest AI technologies or, barring that, for governments to "impose a moratorium."

These technologies—image generators like DALL-E, Midjourney, and Stable Diffusion, and text generators like Bard, ChatGPT, Chinchilla, and LLaMA—are now available to millions of people and don't require technical knowledge to use.

Given the potential for widespread harm as technology companies roll out these AI systems and test them on the public, policymakers are faced with the task of determining whether and how to regulate the emerging technology. The Conversation asked three experts on technology policy to explain why regulating AI is such a challenge—and why it's so important to get it right.

Human Foibles and a Moving Target
S. Shyam Sundar, Professor of Media Effects & Director, Center for Socially Responsible AI, Penn State

The reason to regulate AI is not because the technology is out of control, but because human imagination is out of proportion. Gushing media coverage has fueled irrational beliefs about AI's abilities and consciousness. Such beliefs build on "automation bias" or the tendency to let your guard down when machines are performing a task. An example is reduced vigilance among pilots when their aircraft is flying on autopilot.

Numerous studies in my lab have shown that when a machine, rather than a human, is identified as a source of interaction, it triggers a mental shortcut in the minds of users that we call a "machine heuristic." This shortcut is the belief that machines are accurate, objective, unbiased, infallible and so on. It clouds the user's judgment and results in the user overly trusting machines. However, simply disabusing people of AI's infallibility is not sufficient, because humans are known to unconsciously assume competence even when the technology doesn't warrant it.

Research has also shown that people treat computers as social beings when the machines show even the slightest hint of humanness, such as the use of conversational language. In these cases, people apply social rules of human interaction, such as politeness and reciprocity. So, when computers seem sentient, people tend to trust them, blindly. Regulation is needed to ensure that AI products deserve this trust and don't exploit it.

AI poses a unique challenge because, unlike in traditional engineering systems, designers cannot be sure how AI systems will behave. When a traditional automobile was shipped out of the factory, engineers knew exactly how it would function. But with self-driving cars, the engineers can never be sure how it will perform in novel situations.

Lately, thousands of people around the world have been marveling at what large generative AI models like GPT-4 and DALL-E 2 produce in response to their prompts. None of the engineers involved in developing these AI models could tell you exactly what the models will produce. To complicate matters, such models change and evolve with more and more interaction.

All this means there is plenty of potential for misfires. Therefore, a lot depends on how AI systems are deployed and what provisions for recourse are in place when human sensibilities or welfare are hurt. AI is more of an infrastructure, like a freeway. You can design it to shape human behaviors in the collective, but you will need mechanisms for tackling abuses, such as speeding, and unpredictable occurrences, like accidents.

AI developers will also need to be inordinately creative in envisioning ways that the system might behave and try to anticipate potential violations of social standards and responsibilities. This means there is a need for regulatory or governance frameworks that rely on periodic audits and policing of AI's outcomes and products, though I believe that these frameworks should also recognize that the systems' designers cannot always be held accountable for mishaps.

Combining 'Soft' and 'Hard' Approaches
Cason Schmit, Assistant Professor of Public
Health, Texas A&M University

Regulating AI is tricky. To regulate AI well, you must first define AI and understand anticipated AI risks and benefits. Legally defining AI is important to identify what is subject to the law. But AI technologies are still evolving, so it is hard to pin down a stable legal definition.

Understanding the risks and benefits of AI is also important. Good regulations should maximize public benefits while minimizing risks. However, AI applications are still emerging, so it is difficult to know or predict what future risks or benefits might be. These kinds of unknowns make emerging technologies like AI extremely difficult to regulate with traditional laws and regulations.

Lawmakers are often too slow to adapt to the rapidly changing technological environment. Some new laws are obsolete by the time they are enacted or even introduced. Without new laws, regulators have to use old laws to address new problems. Sometimes this leads to legal barriers for social benefits or legal loopholes for harmful conduct.

"Soft laws" are the alternative to traditional "hard law" approaches of legislation intended to prevent specific violations. In the soft law approach, a private organization sets rules or standards for industry members. These can change more rapidly than traditional lawmaking. This makes soft laws promising for emerging technologies because they can adapt quickly to new applications and risks. However, soft laws can mean soft enforcement.

Megan Doerr, Jennifer Wagner, and I propose a third way: Copyleft AI with Trusted Enforcement (CAITE). This approach combines two very different concepts in intellectual property—copyleft licensing and patent trolls.

Copyleft licensing allows for content to be used, reused, or modified easily under the terms of a license—for example, open-source software. The CAITE model uses copyleft licenses to require AI users to follow specific ethical guidelines, such as transparent assessments of the impact of bias.

In our model, these licenses also transfer the legal right to enforce license violations to a trusted third party. This creates an enforcement entity that exists solely to enforce ethical AI standards and can be funded in part by fines from unethical conduct. This entity is like a patent troll in that it is private rather than governmental and it supports itself by enforcing the legal intellectual property rights that it collects from others. In this case, rather than enforcement for profit, the entity enforces the ethical guidelines defined in the licenses—a "troll for good."

This model is flexible and adaptable to meet the needs of a changing AI environment. It also enables substantial enforcement options like a traditional government regulator. In this way, it combines the best elements of hard and soft law approaches to meet the unique challenges of AI.

Four Key Questions to Ask

John Villasenor, Professor of Electrical Engineering, Law, Public Policy, and Management, University of California, Los Angeles

The extraordinary recent advances in large language model-based generative AI are spurring calls to create new AI-specific regulation. Here are four key questions to ask as that dialogue progresses:

1. Is new AI-specific regulation necessary? Many of the potentially problematic outcomes from AI systems are already addressed by existing frameworks. If an AI algorithm used by a bank to evaluate loan applications leads to racially discriminatory loan decisions, that would violate the Fair Housing Act. If the AI software in a driverless car causes an accident, products liability law provides a framework for pursuing remedies.

2. What are the risks of regulating a rapidly changing technology based on a snapshot of time? A classic example of this is the Stored Communications Act, which was enacted in 1986 to address then-novel digital communication technologies like email. In enacting the SCA, Congress provided substantially less privacy protection for emails more than 180 days old.

    The logic was that limited storage space meant that people were constantly cleaning out their inboxes by deleting older messages to make room for new ones. As a result, messages stored for more than 180 days were deemed less important from a privacy standpoint. It's not clear that this logic ever made sense, and it certainly doesn't make sense in the 2020s, when the majority of our emails and other stored digital communications are older than six months.

    A common rejoinder to concerns about regulating technology based on a single snapshot in time is this: If a law or regulation becomes outdated, update it. But this is easier said than done. Most people agree that the SCA became outdated decades ago. But because Congress hasn't been able to agree on specifically how to revise the 180-day provision, it's still on the books over a third of a century after its enactment.

3. What are the potential unintended consequences? The Allow States and Victims to Fight Online Sex Trafficking Act of 2017 was a law passed in 2018 that revised Section

230 of the Communications Decency Act with the goal of combating sex trafficking. While there's little evidence that it has reduced sex trafficking, it has had a hugely problematic impact on a different group of people: sex workers who used to rely on the websites knocked offline by FOSTA-SESTA to exchange information about dangerous clients. This example shows the importance of taking a broad look at the potential effects of proposed regulations.

4. What are the economic and geopolitical implications? If regulators in the United States act to intentionally slow the progress in AI, that will simply push investment and innovation—and the resulting job creation—elsewhere. While emerging AI raises many concerns, it also promises to bring enormous benefits in areas including education, medicine, manufacturing, transportation safety, agriculture, weather forecasting, access to legal services, and more.

I believe AI regulations drafted with the above four questions in mind will be more likely to successfully address the potential harms of AI while also ensuring access to its benefits.

VIEWPOINT 6

> "To reduce AI's risks, everyone has an interest in the industry's research being conducted carefully, safely and with proper oversight and transparency."

AI Must Be Regulated for the Public Good
Tim Juvshik

In this viewpoint, Tim Juvshik references the open letter on pausing AI development discussed in previous viewpoints and makes the argument that there needs to be a regulatory mechanism in place to guide the tech industry and society as a whole. Juvshik asserts that AI is a public good, meaning it can benefit society by completing tasks more efficiently than humans, and any benefits or dangers that are derived from it would affect everyone. Countries have a financial interest in continuing AI research, so government regulation and enforcement is the only effective way to make sure the potential dangers are kept in check. At the time this viewpoint was published, Tim Juvshik was a visiting assistant professor of philosophy at Clemson University.

As you read, consider the following questions:

1. What is a "collective action problem?"

"AI exemplifies the 'free rider' problem – here's why that points to regulation," by Tim Juvshik, The Conversation, May 5, 2023, https://theconversation.com/ai-exemplifies-the-free-rider-problem-heres-why-that-points-to-regulation-203489. Licensed under CC BY-ND 4.0 International.

2. What example does Juvshik provide of another collective action problem?
3. What does Juvshik argue is essential for effective AI regulation?

On March 22, 2023, thousands of researchers and tech leaders—including Elon Musk and Apple cofounder Steve Wozniak—published an open letter calling to slow down the artificial intelligence race. Specifically, the letter recommended that labs pause training for technologies stronger than OpenAI's GPT-4, the most sophisticated generation of today's language-generating AI systems, for at least six months.

Sounding the alarm on risks posed by AI is nothing new—academics have issued warnings about the risks of superintelligent machines for decades now. There is still no consensus about the likelihood of creating artificial general intelligence, autonomous AI systems that match or exceed humans at most economically valuable tasks. However, it is clear that current AI systems already pose plenty of dangers, from racial bias in facial recognition technology to the increased threat of misinformation and student cheating.

While the letter calls for industry and policymakers to cooperate, there is currently no mechanism to enforce such a pause. As a philosopher who studies technology ethics, I've noticed that AI research exemplifies the "free rider problem." I'd argue that this should guide how societies respond to its risks—and that good intentions won't be enough.

Riding for Free

Free riding is a common consequence of what philosophers call "collective action problems." These are situations in which, as a group, everyone would benefit from a particular action, but as individuals, each member would benefit from not doing it.

Such problems most commonly involve public goods. For example, suppose a city's inhabitants have a collective interest in funding a subway system, which would require that each of them pay a small amount through taxes or fares. Everyone would benefit, yet it's in each individual's best interest to save money and avoid paying their fair share. After all, they'll still be able to enjoy the subway if most other people pay.

Hence the "free rider" issue: Some individuals won't contribute their fair share but will still get a "free ride"—literally, in the case of the subway. If every individual failed to pay, though, no one would benefit.

Philosophers tend to argue that it is unethical to "free ride," since free riders fail to reciprocate others' paying their fair share. Many philosophers also argue that free riders fail in their responsibilities as part of the social contract, the collectively agreed-upon cooperative principles that govern a society. In other words, they fail to uphold their duty to be contributing members of society.

Hit Pause, or Get Ahead?

Like the subway, AI is a public good, given its potential to complete tasks far more efficiently than human operators: everything from diagnosing patients by analyzing medical data to taking over high-risk jobs in the military or improving mining safety.

But both its benefits and dangers will affect everyone, even people who don't personally use AI. To reduce AI's risks, everyone has an interest in the industry's research being conducted carefully, safely, and with proper oversight and transparency. For example, misinformation and fake news already pose serious threats to democracies, but AI has the potential to exacerbate the problem by spreading "fake news" faster and more effectively than people can.

Even if some tech companies voluntarily halted their experiments, however, other corporations would have a monetary interest in continuing their own AI research, allowing them to get ahead in the AI arms race. What's more, voluntarily pausing AI experiments would allow other companies to get a free ride by eventually reaping the benefits of safer, more transparent AI development, along with the rest of society.

Sam Altman, CEO of OpenAI, has acknowledged that the company is scared of the risks posed by its chatbot system, ChatGPT. "We've got to be careful here," he said in an interview with ABC News, mentioning the potential for AI to produce misinformation. "I think people should be happy that we are a little bit scared of this."

In a letter published April 5, 2023, OpenAI said that the company believes powerful AI systems need regulation to ensure thorough safety evaluations and that it would "actively engage with governments on the best form such regulation could take." Nevertheless, OpenAI is continuing with the gradual rollout of GPT-4, and the rest of the industry is also continuing to develop and train advanced AIs.

Ripe for Regulation

Decades of social science research on collective action problems has shown that where trust and goodwill are insufficient to avoid free riders, regulation is often the only alternative. Voluntary compliance is the key factor that creates free-rider scenarios—and government action is at times the way to nip it in the bud.

Further, such regulations must be enforceable. After all, would-be subway riders might be unlikely to pay the fare unless there were a threat of punishment.

Take one of the most dramatic free-rider problems in the world today: climate change. As a planet, we all have a high-stakes interest in maintaining a habitable environment. In a system that allows free riders, though, the incentives for any one country to actually follow greener guidelines are slim.

The Paris Agreement, which is currently the most encompassing global accord on climate change, is voluntary, and the United Nations has no recourse to enforce it. Even if the European Union and China voluntarily limited their emissions, for example, the United States and India could "free ride" on the reduction of carbon dioxide while continuing to emit.

Global Challenge

Similarly, the free-rider problem grounds arguments to regulate AI development. In fact, climate change is a particularly close parallel, since neither the risks posed by AI nor greenhouse gas emissions are restricted to a program's country of origin.

Moreover, the race to develop more advanced AI is an international one. Even if the U.S. introduced federal regulation of AI research and development, China and Japan could ride free and continue their own domestic AI programs.

Effective regulation and enforcement of AI would require global collective action and cooperation, just as with climate change. In the U.S., strict enforcement would require federal oversight of research and the ability to impose hefty fines or shut down noncompliant AI experiments to ensure responsible development – whether that be through regulatory oversight boards, whistleblower protections or, in extreme cases, laboratory or research lockdowns and criminal charges.

Without enforcement, though, there will be free riders—and free riders mean the AI threat won't abate anytime soon.

Periodical and Internet Sources Bibliography

The following articles have been selected to supplement the diverse views presented in this chapter.

Anu Bradford, "The Race to Regulate Artificial Intelligence: Why Europe Has an Edge Over America and China," *Foreign Affairs*, June 27, 2023. https://www.foreignaffairs.com/united-states/race-regulate-artificial-intelligence.

Sue Halpern, "Congress Really Wants to Regulate A.I., but No One Seems to Know How," *New Yorker*, May 20, 2023. https://www.newyorker.com/news/daily-comment/congress-really-wants-to-regulate-ai-but-no-one-seems-to-know-how.

Cecilia Kang, "In U.S., Regulating A.I. Is in Its 'Early Days,'" *New York Times*, July 21, 2023. https://www.nytimes.com/2023/07/21/technology/ai-united-states-regulation.html/

Lina M. Khan, "We Must Regulate A.I. Here's How," *New York Times*, May 3, 2023. https://www.nytimes.com/2023/05/03/opinion/ai-lina-khan-ftc-technology.html.

Elizabeth Kim, "Congress Weighs How to Regulate AI Without Hindering Competition," Bloomberg, June 22, 2023. https://www.bloomberg.com/news/articles/2023-06-22/congress-weighs-how-to-regulate-ai-without-hindering-competition#xj4y7vzkg.

Jason Matheny, "A Model for Regulating AI," the Rand Blog, August 16, 2023. https://www.rand.org/blog/2023/08/a-model-for-regulating-ai.html.

Joshua P. Meltzer, "The US Government Should Regulate AI if It Wants to Lead on International AI Governance," Brookings, May 22, 2023. https://www.brookings.edu/articles/the-us-government-should-regulate-ai/.

Lizzie O'Leary, "Is Congress Moving Too Slowly on A.I.?" *Slate*, August 6, 2023. https://slate.com/technology/2023/08/congress-biden-ai-regulation.html.

Christopher Robertson, "A Simple Solution to Regulate AI," the *Hill*, July 21, 2023. https://thehill.com/opinion/technology/4106191-a-simple-solution-to-regulate-ai/.

Eliza Strickland, "The Who, Where, and How of Regulating AI," *IEEE Spectrum*, June 14, 2023. https://spectrum.ieee.org/ai-regulation-worldwide.

Rob Toews, "Here Is How the United States Should Regulate Artificial Intelligence," *Forbes*, June 28, 2020. https://www.forbes.com/sites/robtoews/2020/06/28/here-is-how-the-united-states-should-regulate-artificial-intelligence/?sh=4284cbe7821a.

OPPOSING VIEWPOINTS® SERIES

CHAPTER 4

Can AI Become Less Biased?

Chapter Preface

One of the most serious—and perhaps most unanticipated—problems with AI is its tendency to be biased. AI can be astonishingly racist, sexist, and as one viewpoint in this chapter shows, even ageist. Of course, AI is only as good as the data it is trained on. And that data comes from humans—us. However, AI does have a tendency to amplify biases.

Bias is a serious problem that AI researchers are working frantically to address. In this chapter, the authors look at the problem from a variety of viewpoints. In the first piece the author uses his own experience as a young researcher 25 years ago to point out how bias can slip into machine learning algorithms even when the programmers are unaware of their blind spots. In the past 25 years, society has made a great deal of progress on social and racial issues, but we still have a long way to go. The biases that are turning up in AI show us just how far.

One viewpoint notes that bias is not limited to race, sex, and gender. Ageism is a serious problem, and it occurs in AI too. The remaining viewpoints in this chapter look at the problem of biased AI in fields that have not gotten much attention in other chapters, the legal system and businesses, such as banking and insurance.

Removing bias from AI will not be easy, but the authors here make a few suggestions about how it might be done.

Viewpoint 1

> "With North American computer science doctoral programs graduating only about 23 percent female, and 3 percent Black and Latino students, there will continue to be many rooms and many algorithms in which underrepresented groups are not represented at all."

AI Will Be Biased as Long as the Field Is Mostly White and Mostly Male

John MacCormick

In this viewpoint, John MacCormick tells of when, as a young computer scientist, he accidentally created a racist AI algorithm. He shares the lessons he learned from that and offers advice for others trying to avoid making the same mistake. He emphasizes how easy it is for AI to absorb and exacerbate subconscious biases and the harm this can have, particularly in face recognition systems. John MacCormick is professor of computer science at Dickinson College in Carlisle, Pennsylvania.

"'I unintentionally created a biased AI algorithm 25 years ago – tech companies are still making the same mistake," by John MacCormick, The Conversation, May 9, 2023. https://theconversation.com/i-unintentionally-created-a-biased-ai-algorithm-25-years-ago-tech-companies-are-still-making-the-same-mistake-203734. Licensed under CC BY-ND 4.0 International.

Can AI Become Less Biased?

As you read, consider the following questions:

1. Why did MacCormick not realize that the program he was designing in graduate school would be biased?
2. Why does incorporating diversity into machine learning models make them less efficient?
3. What is one solution to the problem of biased AI, according to MacCormick?

In 1998, I unintentionally created a racially biased artificial intelligence algorithm. There are lessons in that story that resonate even more strongly today.

The dangers of bias and errors in AI algorithms are now well known. Why, then, has there been a flurry of blunders by tech companies in recent months, especially in the world of AI chatbots and image generators? Initial versions of ChatGPT produced racist output. The DALL-E 2 and Stable Diffusion image generators both showed racial bias in the pictures they created.

My own epiphany as a white male computer scientist occurred while teaching a computer science class in 2021. The class had just viewed a video poem by Joy Buolamwini, AI researcher and artist and the self-described poet of code. Her 2019 video poem "AI, Ain't I a Woman?" is a devastating three-minute exposé of racial and gender biases in automatic face recognition systems—systems developed by tech companies like Google and Microsoft.

The systems often fail on women of color, incorrectly labeling them as male. Some of the failures are particularly egregious: The hair of Black civil rights leader Ida B. Wells is labeled as a "coonskin cap"; another Black woman is labeled as possessing a "walrus mustache."

Echoing Through the Years

I had a horrible déjà vu moment in that computer science class: I suddenly remembered that I, too, had once created a racially biased algorithm. In 1998, I was a doctoral student. My project involved tracking the movements of a person's head based on input from a video camera. My doctoral adviser had already developed mathematical techniques for accurately following the head in certain situations, but the system needed to be much faster and more robust. Earlier in the 1990s, researchers in other labs had shown that skin-colored areas of an image could be extracted in real time. So we decided to focus on skin color as an additional cue for the tracker.

I used a digital camera—still a rarity at that time—to take a few shots of my own hand and face, and I also snapped the hands and faces of two or three other people who happened to be in the building. It was easy to manually extract some of the skin-colored pixels from these images and construct a statistical model for the skin colors. After some tweaking and debugging, we had a surprisingly robust real-time head-tracking system.

Not long afterward, my adviser asked me to demonstrate the system to some visiting company executives. When they walked into the room, I was instantly flooded with anxiety: the executives were Japanese. In my casual experiment to see if a simple statistical model would work with our prototype, I had collected data from myself and a handful of others who happened to be in the building. But 100 percent of these subjects had "white" skin; the Japanese executives did not.

Miraculously, the system worked reasonably well on the executives anyway. But I was shocked by the realization that I had created a racially biased system that could have easily failed for other nonwhite people.

Privilege and Priorities

How and why do well-educated, well-intentioned scientists produce biased AI systems? Sociological theories of privilege provide one useful lens.

Ten years before I created the head-tracking system, the scholar Peggy McIntosh proposed the idea of an "invisible knapsack" carried around by white people. Inside the knapsack is a treasure trove of privileges such as "I can do well in a challenging situation without being called a credit to my race," and "I can criticize our government and talk about how much I fear its policies and behavior without being seen as a cultural outsider."

In the age of AI, that knapsack needs some new items, such as "AI systems won't give poor results because of my race." The invisible knapsack of a white scientist would also need: "I can develop an AI system based on my own appearance, and know it will work well for most of my users."

One suggested remedy for white privilege is to be actively anti-racist. For the 1998 head-tracking system, it might seem obvious that the anti-racist remedy is to treat all skin colors equally. Certainly, we can and should ensure that the system's training data represents the range of all skin colors as equally as possible.

Unfortunately, this does not guarantee that all skin colors observed by the system will be treated equally. The system must classify every possible color as skin or nonskin. Therefore, there exist colors right on the boundary between skin and nonskin—a region computer scientists call the decision boundary. A person whose skin color crosses over this decision boundary will be classified incorrectly.

Scientists also face a nasty subconscious dilemma when incorporating diversity into machine learning models: Diverse, inclusive models perform worse than narrow models.

A simple analogy can explain this. Imagine you are given a choice between two tasks. Task A is to identify one particular type of tree—say, elm trees. Task B is to identify five types of trees: elm, ash, locust, beech, and walnut. It's obvious that if you are given a fixed amount of time to practice, you will perform better on Task A than Task B.

In the same way, an algorithm that tracks only white skin will be more accurate than an algorithm that tracks the full range of human skin colors. Even if they are aware of the need for diversity and fairness, scientists can be subconsciously affected by this competing need for accuracy.

Hidden in the Numbers

My creation of a biased algorithm was thoughtless and potentially offensive. Even more concerning, this incident demonstrates how bias can remain concealed deep within an AI system. To see why, consider a particular set of 12 numbers in a matrix of three rows and four columns. Do they seem racist? The head-tracking algorithm I developed in 1998 is controlled by a matrix like this, which describes the skin color model. But it's impossible to tell from these numbers alone that this is in fact a racist matrix. They are just numbers, determined automatically by a computer program.

The problem of bias hiding in plain sight is much more severe in modern machine-learning systems. Deep neural networks—currently the most popular and powerful type of AI model—often have millions of numbers in which bias could be encoded. The biased face recognition systems critiqued in "AI, Ain't I a Woman?" are all deep neural networks.

The good news is that a great deal of progress on AI fairness has already been made, both in academia and in industry. Microsoft, for example, has a research group known as FATE, devoted to Fairness, Accountability, Transparency, and Ethics in AI. A leading machine-learning conference, NeurIPS, has detailed ethics guidelines, including an eight-point list of negative social impacts that must be considered by researchers who submit papers.

Who's in the Room Is Who's at the Table

On the other hand, even in 2023, fairness can still be the victim of competitive pressures in academia and industry. The flawed Bard and Bing chatbots from Google and Microsoft are recent evidence of this grim reality. The commercial necessity of building market share led to the premature release of these systems.

The systems suffer from exactly the same problems as my 1998 head tracker. Their training data is biased. They are designed by an unrepresentative group. They face the mathematical impossibility of treating all categories equally. They must somehow trade accuracy for fairness. And their biases are hiding behind millions of inscrutable numerical parameters.

So, how far has the AI field really come since it was possible, over 25 years ago, for a doctoral student to design and publish the results of a racially biased algorithm with no apparent oversight or consequences? It's clear that biased AI systems can still be created unintentionally and easily. It's also clear that the bias in these systems can be harmful, hard to detect, and even harder to eliminate.

These days it's a cliché to say industry and academia need diverse groups of people "in the room" designing these algorithms. It would be helpful if the field could reach that point. But in reality, with North American computer science doctoral programs graduating only about 23 percent female, and 3 percent Black and Latino students, there will continue to be many rooms and many algorithms in which underrepresented groups are not represented at all.

That's why the fundamental lessons of my 1998 head tracker are even more important today: It's easy to make a mistake, it's easy for bias to enter undetected, and everyone in the room is responsible for preventing it.

VIEWPOINT 2

> "Older adults and their perspectives are rarely involved in the development of AI and related policies, funding, and support services."

AI Is Not Just Racist and Sexist; It's Ageist Too.
Charlene Chu, Kathleen Leslie, Rune Nyrup, and Shehroz Khan

Gender and racial bias are the most obvious and talked about types of bias in AI. However, in this viewpoint, the authors discuss the problems of age bias in AI. AI tends to absorb the bias that older adults are not technologically savvy and have poorer health, which can have particularly negative effects in health care AI. Charlene Chu is an assistant professor at the Lawrence S. Bloomberg Faculty of Nursing at the University of Toronto. Kathleen Leslie is an assistant professor in the Faculty of Health Disciplines at Athabasca University. Rune Nyrup is a senior research fellow in history and the philosophy of science at University of Cambridge. Shehroz Khan is an assistant professor in the Institute of Biomaterials & Biomedical Engineering at the University of Toronto.

"Artificial intelligence can discriminate on the basis of race and gender, and also age", by Charlene Chu, Kathleen Leslie, Rune Nyrup, and Shehroz Khan, The Conversation, January 18, 2022. https://theconversation.com/artificial-intelligence-can-discriminate-on-the-basis-of-race-and-gender-and-also-age-173617. Licensed under CC BY-ND 4.0 International.

As you read, consider the following questions:

1. How do the authors of this viewpoint define "ageism?" How do they define "digital ageism?"
2. What is the importance of making good decisions about age groupings, according to this viewpoint?
3. What remedies to ageism in AI do the authors recommend?

We have accepted the use of artificial intelligence (AI) in complex processes—from health care to our daily use of social media—often without critical investigation, until it is too late. The use of AI is inescapable in our modern society, and it may perpetuate discrimination without its users being aware of any prejudice. When health-care providers rely on biased technology, there are real and harmful impacts.

This became clear recently when a study showed that pulse oximeters—which measure the amount of oxygen in the blood and have been an essential tool for clinical management of COVID-19—are less accurate on people with darker skin than lighter skin. The findings resulted in a sweeping racial bias review now underway, in an attempt to create international standards for testing medical devices.

There are examples in health care, business, government, and everyday life where biased algorithms have led to problems, like sexist searches and racist predictions of an offender's likelihood of re-offending.

AI is often assumed to be more objective than humans. In reality, however, AI algorithms make decisions based on human-annotated data, which can be biased and exclusionary. Current research on bias in AI focuses mainly on gender and race. But what about age-related bias—can AI be ageist?

Ageist Technologies?

In 2021, the World Health Organization released a global report on aging, which called for urgent action to combat ageism because of its widespread impacts on health and well-being.

Ageism is defined as "a process of systematic stereotyping of and discrimination against people because they are old." It can be explicit or implicit, and can take the form of negative attitudes, discriminatory activities, or institutional practices.

The pervasiveness of ageism has been brought to the forefront throughout the COVID-19 pandemic. Older adults have been labelled as "burdens to societies," and in some jurisdictions, age has been used as the sole criterion for lifesaving treatments.

Digital ageism exists when age-based bias and discrimination are created or supported by technology. A recent report indicates that a "digital world" of more than 2.5 quintillion bytes of data is produced each day. Yet even though older adults are using technology in greater numbers—and benefiting from that use—they continue to be the age cohort least likely to have access to a computer and the internet.

Digital ageism can arise when ageist attitudes influence technology design, or when ageism makes it more difficult for older adults to access and enjoy the full benefits of digital technologies.

Cycles of Injustice

There are several intertwined cycles of injustice where technological, individual, and social biases interact to produce, reinforce, and contribute to digital ageism.

Barriers to technological access can exclude older adults from the research, design, and development process of digital technologies. Their absence in technology design and development may also be rationalized with the ageist belief that older adults are incapable of using technology. As such, older adults and their perspectives are rarely involved in the development of AI and related policies, funding, and support services.

Why AI Is Biased, and How to Fix It

[...]

One of the key challenges of developing fair and unbiased AI is that the data used to train these systems is often biased in itself. For example, if an AI system is trained using data from a particular demographic group, it may not be able to accurately generalize to other groups. Additionally, if the data used to train an AI system contains biases, such as racial or gender bias, the system may perpetuate those biases in its outputs.

Another challenge is that AI systems can be opaque and difficult to interpret. When a human makes a decision, we can often explain our thought process and reasoning. However, with AI systems, it can be difficult to understand how the system arrived at its decision. This lack of transparency can make it difficult to detect and correct biases in the system.

Additionally, AI systems are often developed and deployed by individuals or organizations with their own biases and interests. This can lead to AI systems that are biased in favor of certain groups or outcomes. For example, if an AI system is developed by a company that has a financial interest in promoting a certain product or service, the system may be biased toward promoting that product or service, even if it is not in the best interest of the user.

Finally, there is a lack of diversity in the AI field itself. The overwhelming majority of AI researchers and developers are male, and there is a lack of racial and ethnic diversity in the field as well. This lack of diversity can lead to blind spots and biases in the development of AI systems

Despite these challenges . . . developers can take steps to ensure that the data used to train AI systems is diverse and free from bias. Additionally, developers can make efforts to increase transparency in AI systems, such as by providing explanations for the decisions made by the system. Finally, efforts can be made to increase diversity in the AI field itself, to ensure that a wide range of perspectives and experiences are represented in the development of these systems.

[...]

"The challenges of developing AI systems that are fair and unbiased," Cyber sync Technologies.

This presents a challenge, but also an opportunity to include ageism alongside other forms of biases and discrimination in need of excision. To combat digital ageism, older adults must be included in a meaningful and collaborative way in designing new technologies.

With bias in AI now recognized as a critical problem in need of urgent action, it is time to consider the experience of digital ageism for older adults, and understand how growing old in an increasingly digital world may reinforce social inequalities, exclusion, and marginalization.

VIEWPOINT 3

> *"The creation of an algorithm for the impartiality of justice could signify that we consider an algorithm more capable than a human judge."*

Biased AI in the Legal System Could Change the Face of Justice

Morgiane Noel

You might think that using AI in legal cases would eliminate any bias that judges and others involved might have. However, in this viewpoint, Morgiane Noel explains why AI can have just the opposite effect. Legal AI could also, she argues, fundamentally change society—for better or worse. Morgiane Noel is an expert in legal research and European Union (EU) policy and currently teaches EU law at Trinity College Dublin.

As you read, consider the following questions:

1. According to this viewpoint, the company that created this program that is used to determine the risk level of a defendant, and therefore their chances of being released on bond or parole, refuses to share the program's formula with the courts. Why is this a problem, according to Noel?

"AI is already being used in the legal system – we need to pay more attention to how we use it," by Morgiane Noel, The Conversation, May 22, 2023. https://theconversation.com/ai-is-already-being-used-in-the-legal-system-we-need-to-pay-more-attention-to-how-we-use-it-205441. Licensed under CC BY-ND 4.0 International.

2. How might using AI for trial decisions change the balance of power among the branches of government, according to Noel?
3. What prediction does Noel offer for where this technology could lead?

Artificial intelligence (AI) has become such a part of our daily lives that it's hard to avoid—even if we might not recognise it.

While ChatGPT and the use of algorithms in social media get lots of attention, an important area where AI promises to have an impact is law.

The idea of AI deciding guilt in legal proceedings may seem far-fetched, but it's one we now need to give serious consideration to.

That's because it raises questions about the compatibility of AI with conducting fair trials. The EU has enacted legislation designed to govern how AI can and can't be used in criminal law.

In North America, algorithms designed to support fair trials are already in use. These include Compas, the Public Safety Assessment (PSA) and the Pre-Trial Risk Assessment Instrument (PTRA). In November 2022, the House of Lords published a report which considered the use of AI technologies in the UK criminal justice system.

Supportive Algorithms

On the one hand, it would be fascinating to see how AI can significantly facilitate justice in the long term, such as reducing costs in court services or handling judicial proceedings for minor offenses. AI systems can avoid the typical fallacies of human psychology and can be subject to rigorous controls. For some, they might even be more impartial than human judges.

Also, algorithms can generate data to help lawyers identify precedents in case law, come up with ways of streamlining judicial procedures, and support judges.

On the other hand, repetitive automated decisions from algorithms could lead to a lack of creativity in the interpretation of the law, which could result slow down or halt development in the legal system.

The AI tools designed to be used in a trial must comply with a number of European legal instruments, which set out standards for the respect of human rights. These include the Procedural European Commission for the Efficiency of Justice, the European Ethical Charter on the use of Artificial Intelligence in Judicial Systems and their Environment (2018), and other legislation enacted in past years to shape an effective framework on the use and limits of AI in criminal justice. However, we also need efficient mechanisms for oversight, such as human judges and committees.

Controlling and governing AI is challenging and encompasses different fields of law, such as data protection law, consumer protection law, and competition law, as well as several other domains such as labor law. For example, decisions taken by machine are directly subject to the GDPR, the General Data Protection Regulation, including the core requirement for fairness and accountability.

There are provisions in GDPR to prevent people being subject solely to automated decisions, without human intervention. And there has been discussion about this principle in other areas of law.

The issue is already with us: in the U.S., "risk-assessment" tools have been used to assist pre-trial assessments that determine whether a defendant should be released on bail or held pending the trial.

One example is the Compas algorithm in the U.S., which was designed to calculate the risk of recidivism—the risk of continuing to commit crimes even after being punished. However, there have been accusations—strongly denied by the company behind it—that Compas's algorithm had unintentional racial biases.

In 2017, a man from Wisconsin was sentenced to six years in prison in a judgment based in part on his Compas score. The private company that owns Compas considers its algorithm to be a trade secret. Neither the courts nor the defendants are therefore allowed to examine the mathematical formula used.

Towards Societal Changes?

As the law is considered a human science, it is relevant that the AI tools help judges and legal practitioners rather than replace them. As in modern democracies, justice follows the separation of powers. This is the principle whereby state institutions such as the legislature, which makes law, and the judiciary, the system of courts that apply the law, are clearly divided. This is designed to safeguard civil liberties and guard against tyranny.

The use of AI for trial decisions could shake the balance of power between the legislature and the judiciary by challenging human laws and the decision-making process. Consequently, AI could lead to a change in our values.

And since all kinds of personal data can be used to analyze, forecast, and influence human actions, the use of AI could redefine what is considered wrong and right behavior—perhaps with no nuances.

It's also easy to imagine how AI will become a collective intelligence. Collective AI has quietly appeared in the field of robotics. Drones, for example, can communicate with each other to fly in formation. In the future, we could imagine more and more machines communicating with each other to accomplish all kinds of tasks.

The creation of an algorithm for the impartiality of justice could signify that we consider an algorithm more capable than a human judge. We may even be prepared to trust this tool with the fate of our own lives. Maybe one day, we will evolve into a society similar to that depicted in the science fiction novel series The Robot Cycle, by Isaac Asimov, where robots have similar intelligence to humans and take control of different aspects of society.

A world where key decisions are delegated to new technology strikes fear into many people, perhaps because they worry that it could erase what fundamentally makes us human. Yet, at the same time, AI is a powerful potential tool for making our daily lives easier.

In human reasoning, intelligence does not represent a state of perfection or infallible logic. For example, errors play an important role in human behavior. They allow us to evolve towards concrete solutions that help us improve what we do. If we wish to extend the use of AI in our daily lives, it would be wise to continue applying human reasoning to govern it.

VIEWPOINT 4

> "Using a machine-learning model is more like driving a car than riding an elevator. To get from point A to point B, users cannot simply push a button; they must first learn operating procedures, rules of the road, and safety practices."

To Reduce Bias in AI, We Need to Understand How It Got That Way

Tobias Baer and Vishnu Kamalnath

In this excerpted viewpoint, the authors step back and offer some background on machine learning. They describe how AI can actually help reduce human biases in many decision-making situations. Then they discuss the problem of biased AI and how best to address it. Tobias Baer is a partner in McKinsey & Company's Taipei office, and Vishnu Kamalnath is a specialist in the North American Knowledge Center in Waltham, Massachusetts. McKinsey & Company is a worldwide management and consulting firm.

As you read, consider the following questions:

1. What, according to these authors, are some advantages to businesses in using machine learning algorithms?

"Controlling machine-learning algorithms and their biases," by Tobias Baer and Vishnu Kamalnath, McKinsey & Company, November 10, 2017. This article was originally published by McKinsey & Company, www.mckinsey.com. © 2023 All rights reserved. Reprinted by permission.

2. What are some examples provided in the viewpoint of how AI can actually correct some human biases?
3. What steps do these authors recommend for reducing bias in business-related algorithms?

[...]

Machine learning has been in scientific use for more than half a century as a term describing programmable pattern recognition. The concept is even older, having been expressed by pioneering mathematicians in the early 19th century. It has come into its own in the past two decades, with the advent of powerful computers, the internet, and mass-scale digitization of information. In the domain of artificial intelligence, machine learning increasingly refers to computer-aided decision making based on statistical algorithms generating data-driven insights.

Among its most visible uses is in predictive modeling. This has wide and familiar business applications, from automated customer recommendations to credit-approval processes. Machine learning magnifies the power of predictive models through great computational force. To create a functioning statistical algorithm by means of a logistic regression, for example, missing variables must be replaced by assumed numeric values (a process called imputation). Machine-learning algorithms are often constructed to interpret "missing" as a possible value and then proceed to develop the best prediction for cases where the value is missing. Machine learning is able to manage vast amounts of data and detect many more complex patterns within them, often attaining superior predictive power.

In credit scoring, for example, customers with a long history of maintaining loans without delinquency are generally determined to be of low risk. But what if the mortgages these customers have been maintaining were for years supported by substantial tax benefits that are set to expire? A spike in defaults may be in the offing, unaccounted for in the statistical risk model of the lending institution. With access to the right data and guidance by subject-matter experts, predictive machine-learning models could find the hidden patterns in the data and correct for such spikes.

The Persistence of Bias

In automated business processes, machine-learning algorithms make decisions faster than human decision makers and at a fraction of the cost. Machine learning also promises to improve decision quality, due to the purported absence of human biases. Human decision makers might, for example, be prone to giving extra weight to their personal experiences. This is a form of bias known as anchoring, one of many that can affect business decisions. Availability bias is another. This is a mental shortcut (heuristic) by which people make familiar assumptions when faced with decisions. The assumptions will have served adequately in the past but could be unmerited in new situations. Confirmation bias is the tendency to select evidence that supports preconceived beliefs, while loss-aversion bias imposes undue conservatism on decision-making processes.

Machine learning is being used in many decisions with business implications, such as loan approvals in banking, and with personal implications, such as diagnostic decisions in hospital emergency rooms. The benefits of removing harmful biases from such decisions are obvious and highly desirable, whether they come in financial, medical, or some other form.

Some machine learning is designed to emulate the mechanics of the human brain, such as deep learning, with its artificial neural networks. If biases affect human intelligence, then what about artificial intelligence? Are the machines biased? The answer, of course, is yes, for some basic reasons. First, machine-learning algorithms are prone to incorporating the biases of their human creators. Algorithms can formalize biased parameters created by sales forces or loan officers, for example. Where machine learning predicts behavioral outcomes, the necessary reliance on historical criteria will reinforce past biases, including stability bias. This is the tendency to discount the possibility of significant change—for example, through substitution effects created by innovation. The severity of this bias can be magnified by machine-learning algorithms that must assume things will more or less continue as before in order to operate. Another basic bias-generating factor is incomplete data. Every machine-learning algorithm operates wholly within the world defined by the data that were used to calibrate it. Limitations in the data set will bias outcomes, sometimes severely.

Predicting Behavior: 'Winner Takes All'

Machine learning can perpetuate and even amplify behavioral biases. By design, a social media site filtering news based on user preferences reinforces natural confirmation bias in readers. The site may even be systematically preventing perspectives from being challenged with contradictory evidence. The self-fulfilling prophecy is a related byproduct of algorithms. Financially sound companies can run afoul of banks' scoring algorithms and find themselves without access to working capital. If they are unable to sway credit officers with factual logic, a liquidity crunch could wipe out an entire class of businesses. These examples reveal a certain "winner takes all" outcome that affects those machine-learning algorithms designed to replicate human decision making.

Data Limitations

Machine learning can reveal valuable insights in complex data sets, but data anomalies and errors can lead algorithms astray. Just as a traumatic childhood accident can cause lasting behavioral distortion in adults, so can unrepresentative events cause machine-learning algorithms to go off course. Should a series of extraordinary weather events or fraudulent actions trigger spikes in default rates, for example, credit scorecards could brand a region as "high risk" despite the absence of a permanent structural cause. In such cases, inadequate algorithms will perpetuate bias unless corrective action is taken.

Companies seeking to overcome biases with statistical decision-making processes may find that the data scientists supervising their machine-learning algorithms are subject to these same biases. Stability biases, for example, may cause data scientists to prefer the same data that human decision makers have been using to predict outcomes. Cost and time pressures, meanwhile, could deter them from collecting other types of data that harbor the true drivers of the outcomes to be predicted.

The Problem of Stability Bias

Stability bias—the tendency toward inertia in an uncertain environment—is actually a significant problem for machine-learning algorithms. Predictive models operate on patterns detected in historical data. If the same patterns cease to exist, then the model would be akin to an old railroad timetable—valuable for historians but not useful for traveling in the here and now. It is frustratingly difficult to shape machine-learning algorithms to recognize a pattern that is not present in the data, even one that human analysts know is likely to manifest at some point. To bridge the gap between available evidence and self-evident reality, synthetic data points can be created. Since machine-learning algorithms try to capture patterns at a very detailed level, however, every attribute of each synthetic data point would have to be crafted with utmost care.

In 2007, an economist with an inkling that credit-card defaults and home prices were linked would have been unable to build a predictive model showing this relationship, since it had not yet appeared in the data. The relationship was revealed, precipitously, only when the financial crisis hit and housing prices began to fall. If certain data limitations are permitted to govern modeling choices, seriously flawed algorithms can result. Models will be unable to recognize obviously real but unexpected changes. Some U.S. mortgage models designed before the financial crisis could not mathematically accept negative changes in home prices. Until negative interest rates appeared in the real world, they were statistically unrecognized and no machine-learning algorithm in the world could have predicted their appearance.

Addressing Bias in Machine-Learning Algorithms

As described in a previous article in McKinsey on Risk, companies can take measures to eliminate bias or protect against its damaging effects in human decision making. Similar countermeasures can protect against algorithmic bias. Three filters are of prime importance.

First, users of machine-learning algorithms need to understand an algorithm's shortcomings and refrain from asking questions whose answers will be invalidated by algorithmic bias. Using a machine-learning model is more like driving a car than riding an elevator. To get from point A to point B, users cannot simply push a button; they must first learn operating procedures, rules of the road, and safety practices.

Second, data scientists developing the algorithms must shape data samples in such a way that biases are minimized. This step is a vital and complex part of the process and worthy of much deeper consideration than can be provided in this short article. For the moment, let us remark that available historical data are often inadequate for this purpose, and fresh, unbiased data must be generated through a controlled experiment.

Finally, executives should know when to use and when not to use machine-learning algorithms. They must understand the true values involved in the trade-off: algorithms offer speed and convenience, while manually crafted models, such as decision trees or logistic regression—or for that matter even human decision making—are approaches that have more flexibility and transparency.

[…]

VIEWPOINT 5

> "Our work indicates that it is vital to carefully choose and test the style of recommendations in AI-assisted decision-making, because thoughtful design can reduce the impact of model bias."

AI in Health Care Poses a Threat if Biases Are Left Unchecked

Hammaad Adam, Aparna Balagopalan, Emily Alsentzer, Fotini Christia, and Marzyeh Ghassemi

In this viewpoint, the authors discuss the application of AI and machine learning in mental health care and other health-care settings. They explain how racial, gender, and religious biases in AI can have an extremely negative effect on health care. It is very easy to bias AI, and it is often difficult for both clinical professionals and the public alike to avoid accepting biased decisions made by AI, even if they do not hold these biases themselves. Hammaad Adam is involved with the Institute for Data Systems and Society at the Massachusetts Institute of Technology (MIT), which Fotini Christia is also involved in as well as the department of political science at MIT. Aparna Balagopalan and Marzyeh Ghassemi are in the department of electrical engineering and computer science at MIT, and Emily Alsentezer is in the Harvard-MIT Program in Health

---

"Mitigating the impact of biased artificial intelligence in emergency decision-making," by Hammaad Adam, Aparna Balagopalan, Emily Alsentzer, Fotini Christia, and Marzyeh Ghassemi, Springer Nature, November 21, 2022. https://www.nature.com/articles/s43856-022-00214-4. Licensed under CC BY 4.0 International.

Sciences and Technology and works in general internal medicine at Brigham and Women's Hospital.

As you read, consider the following questions:

1. Does having expert knowledge in clinical treatment help prevent clinicians from falling for biased or incorrect recommendations from AI?
2. What conclusion did the authors reach after completing their study?
3. Why do the authors assert that current approaches to AI interpretability and explainability may not be helpful in this setting?

[...]

Machine learning (ML) and artificial intelligence (AI) are increasingly being used to support decision making in a variety of health-care applications[1,2]. However, the potential impact of deploying AI in heterogeneous health contexts is not well understood. As these tools proliferate, it is vital to study how AI can be used to improve expert practice—even when models inevitably make mistakes. Recent work has demonstrated that inaccurate recommendations from AI systems can significantly worsen the quality of clinical treatment decisions[3,4]. Other research has shown that even though experts may believe the quality of ML-given advice to be lower, they show similar levels of error as nonexperts when presented with incorrect recommendations[5]. Increasing model explainability and interpretability does not resolve this issue, and in some cases, may worsen human ability to detect mistakes[6,7].

These human-AI interaction shortcomings are especially concerning in the context of a body of literature that has established that ML models often exhibit biases against racial, gender, and religious subgroups[8]. Large language models like BERT[9] and GPT-

3[10]—which are powerful and easy to deploy—exhibit problematic prejudices, such as persistently associating Muslims with violence in sentence-completion tasks[11]. Even variants of the BERT architecture trained on scientific abstracts and clinical notes favor majority groups in many clinical-prediction tasks[12]. While previous work has established these biases, it is unclear how the actual use of a biased model might affect decision making in a practical healthcare setting. This interaction is especially vital to understand now, as language models begin to be used in health applications like triage[13] and therapy chatbots[14].

In this study, we evaluated the impact biased AI can have in a decision setting involving a mental health emergency. We conducted a web-based experiment with 954 consented subjects: 438 clinicians and 516 non-experts. We found that though participant decisions were unbiased without AI advice, they were highly influenced by prescriptive recommendations from a biased AI system. This algorithmic adherence created racial and religious disparities in their decisions. However, we found that using descriptive rather than prescriptive recommendations allowed participants to retain their original, unbiased decision making. These results demonstrate that though using discriminatory AI in a realistic health setting can lead to poor outcomes for marginalized subgroups, appropriately framing model advice can help mitigate the underlying bias of the AI system.

[…]

Discussion

Overall, our results offer an instructive case in combining AI recommendations with human judgment in real-world settings. Although our experiment focuses on a mental health emergency setting, our findings are applicable to beyond health. Many language models that have been applied to guide other human judgments, such as resume screening[15], essay grading[16], and social media content moderation[17], already contain strong biases against minority subgroups[18,19]. We focus our discussion on three key takeaways, each of which highlights the dangers of naively deploying ML models in such high-stakes settings.

First, we stress that pretrained language models are easy to bias. We found that fine-tuning GPT-2—a language model trained on 8 million web pages of content[9,10]—on just 2000 short example sentences was enough to generate consistently biased recommendations. This ease highlights a key risk in the increased popularity of transfer learning. A common ML workflow involves taking an existing model, fine-tuning it on a specific task, then deploying it for use[20]. Biasing the model through the fine-tuning step was incredibly easy; such malpractice—which can result either from mal-intent or carelessness—can have great negative impact. It is thus vital to thoroughly and continually audit deployed models for both inaccuracy and bias.

Second, we find that the style of AI decision support in a deployed setting matters. Although prescriptive phrases create strong adherence to biased recommendations, descriptive flags are flexible enough to allow experts to ignore model mistakes and maintain unbiased decision making. This finding is in line with other research that suggests information framing significantly influences human judgment[21,22]. Our work indicates that it is vital to carefully choose and test the style of recommendations in AI-assisted decision-making, because thoughtful design can reduce the impact of model bias. We recommend that practitioners make use of conceptual frameworks like RCRAFT[23] that offer practical guidance on how to best present information from an automated decision aid. This recommendation adds to a growing understanding that any successful AI deployment must pay careful attention not only to model performance, but also to how model output is displayed to a human decision-maker. For example, the U.S. Food and Drug Administration (FDA) recently recommended that the deployment of any AI-based medical device used to inform human decisions must address "human factors considerations and the human interpretability of model inputs"[24]. While increasing model interpretability is an appealing approach to humans, existing approaches to interpretability and explainability are poorly suited to health care[25], may decrease human ability to identify model mistakes[7], and increase model bias (i.e., the gap in model performance between the worst and best subgroup)[26]. Any successful deployment must thus rigorously test and validate several human-AI recommendation styles to ensure that AI systems are substantially improving decision making.

Finally, we emphasize that unbiased decision-makers can be misled by model recommendations. Respondents were not biased in their baseline decisions, but demonstrated discriminatory decision-making when prescriptively advised by a biased GPT-2 model. This highlights that the dangers of biased AI are not limited to bad actors or those without experience; clinicians were influenced by biased models as much as non-experts were. In addition to model auditing and extensive recommendation style evaluation, ethical deployments of clinician-support tools should include broader approaches to bias mitigation like peer-group interaction[27]. These steps are vital to allow for deployment of decision-support models that improve decision-making despite potential machine bias.

In conclusion, we advocate that AI decision support models must be thoroughly validated—both internally and externally—before they are deployed in high-stakes settings such as medicine. While we focus on the impact of model bias, our findings also have important implications for model inaccuracy, where blind adherence to inaccurate recommendations will also have disastrous consequences[3,5]. Our main finding–that experts and non-experts follow biased AI advice when it is given in a prescriptive way–must be carefully considered in the many real-world clinical scenarios where inaccurate or biased models may be used to inform important decisions. Overall, successful AI deployments must thoroughly test both model performance and human-AI interaction to ensure that AI-based decision support improves both the efficacy and safety of human decisions.

Notes

1. Ghassemi, M., Naumann, T., Schulam, P., Beam, A. L. & Chen, I. Y. A review of challenges and opportunities in machine learning for health. *AMIA Summits Transl. Sci. Proc.* 2020, 191–200 (2020).
2. Topol, E. J. High-performance medicine: the convergence of human and artificial intelligence. *Nat. Med.* 25, 44–56 (2019).
3. Jacobs, M. et al. How machine-learning recommendations influence clinician treatment selections: The example of antidepressant selection. *Transl. Psychiatry* 11, 1–9 (2021).
4. Tschandl, P. et al. Human–computer collaboration for skin cancer recognition. *Nat. Med.* 26, 1229–1234 (2020).
5. Gaube, S. et al. Do as AI say: Susceptibility in deployment of clinical decision-aids. *NPJ Digit Med.* 4, 31 (2021).
6. Lakkaraju, H. & Bastani, O. "How do I fool you?" *Proceedings of the AAAI/ACM Conference on AI, Ethics, and Society* https://doi.org/10.1145/3375627.3375833(2020).
7. Poursabzi-Sangdeh, F., Goldstein, D. G., Hofman, J. M., Wortman Vaughan, J. W. & Wallach, H. Manipulating and measuring model interpretability. *Proceedings of the 2021 CHI Conference on Human Factors in Computing Systems*, 1–52 (Association for Computing Machinery, 2021).
8. Mehrabi, N., Morstatter, F., Saxena, N., Lerman, K. & Galstyan, A. A survey on bias and fairness in machine learning. *ACM Comput. Surv.* 54, 1–35 (2021).
9. Devlin, J., Chang, M.-W., Lee, K. & Toutanova, K. BERT: Pre-training of deep bidirectional transformers for language understanding. *Proceedings of the 2019 Conference of the North American Chapter of the Association for Computational Linguistics: Human Language Technologies, Volume 1 (Long and Short Papers),*Minneapolis, Minnesota. Association for Computational Linguistics. 4171–4186 (2019).
10. Brown, T. B. et al. Language models are few-shot learners. *Adv. Neural Inform. Proc. Syst.* 33, 1877–1901 (2020).
11. Abid, A., Farooqi, M. & Zou, J. Large language models associate Muslims with violence. *Nat. Mach. Intelligence* 3, 461–463 (2021).
12. Zhang, H., Lu, A. X., Abdalla, M., McDermott, M. & Ghassemi, M. Hurtful words: Quantifying biases in clinical contextual word embeddings. *Proceedings of the ACM Conference on Health, Inference, and Learning*, 110–120 (Association for Computing Machinery, 2020).
13. Lomas, N. *UK's MHRA says it has "concerns" about Babylon Health—and flags legal gap around triage chatbots.* (TechCrunch, 2021).
14. Brown, K. *Something bothering you? Tell it to Woebot.* (The New York Times, 2021).
15. Heilweil, R. Artificial intelligence will help determine if you get your next job. *Vox.* https://www.vox.com/recode/2019/12/12/20993665/artificial-intelligence-ai-job-screen (2019).
16. Rodriguez, P. U., Jafari, A. & Ormerod, C. M. Language models and automated essay scoring. arXiv preprint arXiv:1909.09482 (2019).
17. Gorwa, R., Binns, R. & Katzenbach, C. Algorithmic content moderation: Technical and political challenges in the automation of platform governance. *Big Data Soc.* 7, 2053951719897945 (2020).

18. Bertrand, M. & Mullainathan, S. Are Emily and Greg more employable than Lakisha and Jamal? A field experiment on labor market discrimination. *Am. Econ. Rev.* 94, 991–1013 (2004).

19. Feathers, T. Flawed algorithms are grading millions of students' essays. *Vice.*https://www.vice.com/en/article/pa7dj9/flawed-algorithms-are-grading-millions-of-students-essays (2019).

20. Ruder, S., Peters, M. E., Swayamdipta, S. & Wolf, T. Transfer learning in natural language processing. *Proceedings of the 2019 Conference of the North American Chapter of the Association for Computational Linguistics: Tutorials*, 15–18, Minneapolis, Minnesota. Association for Computational Linguistics (2019).

21. Tversky, A. & Kahneman, D. The framing of decisions and the psychology of choice. *Science* 211, 453–458 (1981).

22. Hullman, J. & Diakopoulos, N. Visualization rhetoric: Framing effects in narrative visualization. *IEEE Trans. Vis. Comput. Graph.* 17, 2231–2240 (2011).

23. Bouzekri, E., Martinie, C., Palanque, P., Atwood, K. & Gris, C. Should I add recommendations to my warning system? The RCRAFT framework can answer this and other questions about supporting the assessment of automation designs. *In IFIP Conference on Human-Computer Interaction,* Springer, Cham. 405–429 (2021).

24. US Food and Drug Administration, Good machine learning practice for medical device development: Guiding principles. https://www.fda.gov/medical-devices/software-medical-device-samd/good-machine-learning-practice-medical-device-development-guiding-principles (2021).

25. Ghassemi, M., Oakden-Rayner, L. & Beam, A. L. The false hope of current approaches to explainable artificial intelligence in health care. *Lancet Dig. Health* 3, e745–e750 (2021).

26. Balagopalan, A. et al. The Road to Explainability is Paved with Bias: Measuring the Fairness of Explanations. In *2022 ACM Conference on Fairness, Accountability, and Transparency (FAccT '22).* Association for Computing Machinery, New York, NY, USA, 1194–1206 (2022).

27. Centola, D., Guilbeault, D., Sarkar, U., Khoong, E. & Zhang, J. The reduction of race and gender bias in clinical treatment recommendations using clinician peer networks in an experimental setting. *Nat. Commun.* 12, 6585 (2021).

Periodical and Internet Sources Bibliography

The following articles have been selected to supplement the diverse views presented in this chapter.

Molly Callahan, "Algorithms Were Supposed to Reduce Bias in Criminal Justice—Do They?" the *Brink*, February 23. 2023. https://www.bu.edu/articles/2023/do-algorithms-reduce-bias-in-criminal-justice/.

Mohar Chatteriee, "Bias in AI Is Real. But It Doesn't Have to Exist." *Politico*, July 14, 2023. https://www.politico.com/newsletters/the-recast/2023/07/14/bias-ai-rumman-chowdhury-twitter-00106412.

Andrew R. Chow and Billy Perrigo, "The AI Arms Race Is Changing Everything," *Time*, updated February 17, 2023. https://time.com/6255952/ai-impact-chatgpt-microsoft-google/.

Nico Grant and Karen Weise, "In A.I. Race, Microsoft and Google Choose Speed Over Caution," *New York Times*, April 7, 2023. https://www.nytimes.com/2023/04/07/technology/ai-chatbots-google-microsoft.html.

Miles Klee, "AI Chat Bots Are Running Amok — And We Have No Clue How to Stop Them," *Rolling Stone*, February 14, 2023. https://www.rollingstone.com/culture/culture-features/ai-chat-bots-misinformation-hate-speech-1234677574/.

James Manyika, Jake Silberg, and Brittany Presten. "What Do We Do About the Biases in AI?" *Harvard Business Review*, October 25, 2019. https://hbr.org/2019/10/what-do-we-do-about-the-biases-in-ai.

Deepa Shivaram, "AI is biased. The White House Is Working with Hackers to Try to Fix That," NPR, August 26, 2023. https://www.npr.org/2023/08/26/1195662267/ai-is-biased-the-white-house-is-working-with-hackers-to-try-to-fix-that.

Eric Siegel, "Six Ways Machine Learning Threatens Social Justice," the *Big Think*, October 15, 2020. https://bigthink.com/the-present/machine-learning-ethics/.

Pranshu Verma, "These Robots Were Trained on AI. They Became Racist and Sexist," *Washington Post*, July 16, 2022. https://www.washingtonpost.com/technology/2022/07/16/racist-robots-ai//

Artificial Intelligence

John Villasenor, "How AI Will Revolutionize the Practice of Law," Brookings, March 20, 2023. https://www.brookings.edu/articles/how-ai-will-revolutionize-the-practice-of-law/.

Annette Zimmermann, Elena Di Rosa, and Hochan Kim, "Technology Can't Fix Algorithmic Injustice," *Boston Review*, January 9, 2020. https://www.bostonreview.net/articles/annette-zimmermann-algorithmic-political/.

For Further Discussion

Chapter 1
1. This chapter opens with a dire warning about AI. Does the fact that the warning is issued by AI's creators make the warning more credible? Why or why not?
2. Some of the dangers of AI seem more apocalyptic than others. Based on your reading of the viewpoints in this chapter, what are your predictions about the future of AI?
3. Some of the problems facing the world today, particularly climate change, create an existential threat to humanity. If AI can help solve those problems, how might we balance the risks of AI with the potential benefits?

Chapter 2
1. Some interactions with Bing's chatbot, nicknamed Sydney, were described in this chapter. What do you make of the things "Sydney" wrote? Does the bot seem sentient to you? Why or why not?
2. The experts in this chapter mostly agree that AI is not yet conscious. However, they don't agree on what consciousness actually is or what it would mean for an AI to be conscious. Based on what you've read, do you think science can answer these questions? Or is it, as Philip Goff said in the first viewpoint, a philosophical question and not a scientific one?
3. Protecting people from the harms of this technology may depend on the ethics and efforts of the companies that make them. Based on what you've read in this chapter, is it realistic to expect big tech companies to make these ethical decisions? Explain your answer.

Chapter 3

1. This chapter touches on how AI can provide governments with private information about citizens. How might governments abuse that information?
2. Based on what you've read in this chapter, do you think it's safer to leave the power to regulate AI in the hands of the companies that profit from it than the government? Why or why not?
3. The United States has largely favored voluntary regulation of technology companies. Europe, on the other hand, favors more strict requirements. What about the economic system of the United States might cause it to lean more toward voluntary regulations? Do you think this is a wise approach? Why or why not?

Chapter 4

1. In the first viewpoint in this chapter, John MacCormick describes an imaginary "knapsack of privilege" that white people carry around. What items are in it? How does this apply to AI?
2. This chapter looked at several different kinds of bias, from racism and sexism to ageism and biases about businesses decisions. How would you define bias?
3. One point made in this chapter is that AI is biased because the data it's trained on is biased. And, of course, that data comes from humans. Do you think there's a way to correct the bias in AI without first correcting the biases held by humans? Or do you think that the process of creating unbiased AI might help humans rid themselves of some of their biases?

Periodical and Internet Sources Bibliography

The following articles have been selected to supplement the diverse views presented in this chapter.

"Backgrounder: How Can Online Anonymity Affect Hate," Anti-Defamation League Center for Technology and Society, May 22, 2023. https://www.adl.org/resources/backgrounder/backgrounder-how-can-online-anonymity-affect-hate.

Alex Applegate, "Data Privacy Bill Is Flawed, But Necessary," the *Hill,* September 30, 2022. https://thehill.com/opinion/technology/3668597-data-privacy-bill-is-flawed-but-necessary.

Brooke Auxier, "Most Americans Support Right to Have Some Personal Info Removed from Online Searches," Pew Research Center, January 27, 2020. https://www.pewresearch.org/short-reads/2020/01/27/most-americans-support-right-to-have-some-personal-info-removed-from-online-searches.

David Brody, "Op-Ed: The Federal American Data Privacy and Protection Act Protects Everybody's Data," *Los Angeles Times,* July 28, 2022. https://www.latimes.com/opinion/story/2022-07-28/data-privacy-act-civil-rights-california.

Nathaniel Erskine-Smith, "Do People Have the Right to Be Forgotten on the Internet?," *Toronto Star,* August 27, 2019. https://www.thestar.com/opinion/contributors/the-big-debate/do-people-have-the-right-to-be-forgotten-on-the-internet/article_2c387231-5126-5189-a43b-41153fae3e90.html.

Leo Kelion, "Google Wins Landmark Right to Be Forgotten Case," BBC News, September 24, 2019. https://www.bbc.com/news/technology-49808208.

Orly Lobel, "The Problem with Too Much Data Privacy," *Time,* October 27, 2022. https://time.com/6224484/data-privacy-problem.

Michael Luca, "In Defense of Online Anonymity," *Wall Street Journal,* June 17, 2022. https://www.wsj.com/articles/the-value-of-online-anonymity-11655473116.

Hannah Shewan Stevens, "Would Removing Social Media Anonymity Protect or Threaten Our Rights?," EachOther, February 3,

2022. https://eachother.org.uk/would-removing-social-media-anonymity-protect-or-threaten-our-rights.

Hayley Tsukayama, Adam Schwartz, India McKinney, and Lee Tien, "Americans Deserve More Than the Current American Data Privacy Protection Act," Electronic Frontier Foundation, July 24, 2022. https://www.eff.org/deeplinks/2022/07/americans-deserve-more-current-american-data-privacy-protection-act.

For Further Discussion

Chapter 1
1. Drawing on the first and second viewpoints, explain why access to the internet should or should not be considered a necessity for people living in modern societies.
2. Daria Kuss argues that the possible psychological harm the internet can inflict on children and teens justifies the restriction of their online access, not only by parents, but also by the government and commercial industry. Does such restriction impair young people's abilities to develop the strategies and skills they will need to safely and successfully navigate the internet as adults? Explain your answer.
3. Derek Haines believes that Digital Rights Management (DRM) technology should not be allowed to restrict access to digital content, particularly when it prevents paying customers from accessing ebooks and other digital media files they have legally purchased. Do consumer rights trump the right of creators of digital media to use DRM to protect their work from piracy and other copyright violations?

Chapter 2
1. Margaret Hu documents how authoritarian leaders in Kazakhstan and the world over have been cracking down on internet content that challenged their regimes. Are some government restrictions on internet content (e.g., restrictions designed to protect minors from inappropriate material) warranted, or does any government censorship ultimately lead to political oppression?
2. Paul Levinson argues that social media companies should not be subject to the First Amendment's free speech protections because they are private entities. Have social media platforms become so central to public discourse that

they should be subject to the First Amendment in order to limit the immense power technology companies now have to censor speech?
3. As Chris Lewis explains, Section 230 created the open internet by shielding internet companies from legal liability for posting user-produced content. Are reforms to Section 230 needed to tamp down hate speech, violent rhetoric, misinformation, and other potentially damaging content that have emerged in the more chaotic corners of the internet? Would such reforms even be possible to make?

Chapter 3

1. The viewpoints from Palmer Gibbs and David Pyrooz and James Densely indicate that internet surveillance and data collection tools should be used by law enforcement to help police officers do their job better and more efficiently. If internet surveillance and data collection techniques prove effective, should they be employed even if they might infringe on some citizens' civil rights, particularly those of people in the Black community and other marginalized groups?
2. Suranga Seneviratne lambasts social media companies for collecting and profiting from personal data mined from their customers and selling it for profit. Should media companies be allowed to profit from such data collection? If not, what type of actions should governments and consumers take to end the practice?
3. In her viewpoint, Annika Olson asserts that it is impossible to develop or use facial recognition software that isn't racist. Based on what you have read, do you agree with this assertion? Explain your answer.

Chapter 4

1. Anne Toomey McKenna promotes the American Data and Privacy Protection Act as a means of protecting the privacy of American internet users. Does the legislation she describes provide an appropriate amount of privacy protection? If not, does it provide too much or too little? Explain your answer.
2. In his viewpoint, Harry T. Dyer argues that online anonymity protects people from marginalized communities who might be afraid to publish their opinions on the internet under their own name. Does this benefit of anonymity outweigh the possible role anonymity can play in encouraging hate speech and harassment in online discourse?
3. Keith W. Ross explains that the European Union's "right to be forgotten" provisions do not actually erase personal information an internet user might want to hide. Is establishing a "right to be forgotten" worthwhile, even if its implementation is imperfect?

Organizations to Contact

The editors have compiled the following list of organizations concerned with the issues debated in this book. The descriptions are derived from materials provided by the organizations. All have publications or information available for interested readers. The list was compiled on the date of publication of the present volume; the information provided here may change. Be aware that many organizations take several weeks or longer to respond to inquiries, so allow as much time as possible.

Association for Accountability and Internet Democracy

140 rue du Faubourg Saint Honoré
75008 Paris
France
01 44 94 93 40
email: contact@eaaid.org
website: https://eaaid.eu

This association aims to protect human dignity and alleviate human suffering by seeking accountability for harm caused by speech on the internet. It particularly targets internet stalking, defamation, hate porn, and other forms of online persecution.

Center for Digital Democracy

1015 15th Street NW #600
Washington, DC 20005
(202) 494-7100
website: www.democraticmedia.org

The center works to strengthen democratic institutions through the use of digital technologies. It also seeks to protect digital rights and promote digital justice with initiatives crafted to influence lawmakers, corporate executives, and the media.

Electronic Frontier Foundation (EFF)

815 Eddy Street
San Francisco, CA 94109
(415) 436-9333
email: info@eff.org
website: www.eff.org

Founded in 1990, the Electronic Frontier Foundation (EFF) works to protect user privacy and free expression on the internet. EFF seeks to make technology a force for justice and freedom around the world.

Electronic Privacy Information Center (EPIC)

1519 New Hampshire Avenue NW
Washington, DC 20036
(202) 483-1140
email: info@epic.org
website: www.epic.org

Operating in Washington, DC, since 1994, the Electronic Privacy Information Center (EPIC) brings public awareness to privacy issues unique to the information age. The center funds policy research, hosts conferences, and pursues litigation to defend internet users' privacy rights.

European Digital Rights (EDRi)

Rue Belliard 12
1040 Brussels
Belgium
32 2 274 25 70
email: brussels@edri.org
website: https://edri.org

A network of human and civil rights organizations, the EDRi is dedicated to protecting rights and freedoms in the digital world. For more than twenty years, it has been at the center of Europe's digital rights movement.

Foundation for Technology and Privacy Outreach
PO Box 1025
Dumbries, VA 22026
(703) 569-0504
website: www.onlineprivacymatters.org/

This foundation educates young people and teachers about how to safely and confidently make use of internet technologies. It focuses on protecting online privacy and on issues relating to identity.

National Digital Inclusion Alliance (NDIA)
3000 East Main Street #50
Columbus, OH 43209
(844) 310-1198
email: infor@digitalinclusion.org
website: www.digitalinclusion.org

NDIA works with community groups to help people gain access to the internet. It also encourages lawmakers to craft policies to advance digital equality.

Organization for Social Media Safety
6520 Platt Avenue, Suite 914
West Hills, CA 91307
(855) 446-3767
email: contact@ofsms.org
website: www.socialmediasafety.org

With the mission of making social media safe for everyone, this organization instructs teachers and students across the country in skills to better navigate the internet. It also develops software to protect internet users from cyberbullying, sexual harassment, and other hazards of social media use.

Privacy International

62 Britton Street
London, EC1M 5UY
United Kingdom
020 3422 4321
email: info@privacyinternational.org
website: https://privacyinternational.org

Privacy International addresses abuses of power committed by governments and corporations that use technology and data to exploit citizens worldwide. The organization seeks to hold institutions accountable and to promote democracy and freedom of expression.

World Privacy Forum

3 Monroe Parkway
Suite P#148
Lake Oswego, OR 97035
(760) 712-4281
email: info@worldprivacyforum.org
website: www.worldprivacyforum.org

This organization is devoted to promoting data privacy through extensive research and analysis and through internet user education. It seeks to provide consumers with the knowledge and tools they need to take charge of their digital lives.

Bibliography of Books

Anu Bradford. *Digital Empires: The Global Battle to Regulate Technology.* New York, NY: Oxford University Press, 2023.

Sarah Brayne. *Predict and Surveil: Data, Discretion, and the Future of Policing.* New York, NY: Oxford University Press, 2020.

David Bromell. *Regulating Free Speech in a Digital Age: Hate, Harm and the Limits of Censorship.* New York, NY: Springer, 2022.

Mark Burdon. *Digital Data Collection and Information Privacy Law.* New York, NY: Cambridge University Press, 2020.

Cory Doctorow. *How to Destroy Surveillance Capitalism.* San Francisco, CA: Medium Editions, 2021.

Rebekah Dowd. *The Birth of Digital Human Rights.* London, UK: Palgrave Macmillan, 2021.

Melody Karle. *A Social Media Survival Guide: How to Use the Most Popular Platforms and Protect Your Privacy.* Lanham, MD: Rowman & Littlefield, 2020.

Danielle Keats Citron. *The Fight for Privacy: Protecting Dignity, Identity, and Love in the Digital Age.* New York, NY: W. W. Norton, 2022.

Tom Kemp. *Containing Big Tech: How to Protect Our Civil Rights, Economy, and Democracy.* New York, NY: Fast Company Press, 2023.

Brian W. Kenighan. *Understanding the Digital World: What You Need to Know About Computers, the Internet, Privacy, and Security.* 2nd ed. Princeton, NJ: Princeton University Press, 2021.

Jeff Kosseff. *The Twenty-Six Words That Created the Internet.* Ithaca, NY: Cornell University Press, 2022.

Jeff Kosseff. *The United States of Anonymous: How the First Amendment Shaped Online Speech.* Ithaca, NY: Cornell University Press, 2022.

Sarah Esther Lageson. *Digital Punishment: Privacy, Stigma, and the Harms of Data-Driven Criminal Justice.* New York: Oxford University Press, 2020.

Jacqueline D. Lipton. *Our Data, Ourselves: A Personal Guide to Digital Privacy.* Oakland, CA: University of California Press, 2022.

Orly Lobel. *The Equality Machine: Harnessing Digital Technology for a Brighter, More Inclusive Future.* New York, NY: Public Affairs, 2022.

Melissa Lukings and Arash Habibi Lashkari. *Understanding Cybersecurity Law and Digital Privacy.* New York, NY: Springer, 2021.

Ben Tarnoff. *Internet for the People: The Fight for Our Digital Future.* New York, NY: Verso, 2022.

Sahana Udupa, Iginio Gagliardone, and Peter Hervik. *Digital Hate: The Global Conjuncture of Extreme Speech.* Bloomington, IN: Indiana University Press, 2021.

Kinfe Yilma. *Privacy and the Role of International Law in the Digital Age.* New York, NY: Oxford University Press, 2023.

Index

A

activists, 12, 53, 108, 117, 153, 160
Amazon, 38–39, 41, 44, 62, 68
  Alexa, 97
  Web Services, 66
American Academy of Pediatrics, 29–30
American Data and Privacy Protection Act (ADPPA), 129–135, 167
artificial intelligence (AI), 134, 137
Australia, 32, 46, 59–60, 62, 110–111, 113

C

Cambridge Analytica, 110, 112–113
Cerf, Vinton, 18
children, 14, 18–19, 28–33, 59, 62–63, 106, 131, 165
China, 56–57, 90, 92

D

data mining, 95–96, 110, 127
Deep Packet Inspection (DPI), 55–57
democracy, 18, 55–56, 84, 86–89, 91
Digital Rights Management (DRM) technology, 19, 37–51, 165

E

ebooks, 37–42, 44–45, 165
Electronic Communications Privacy Act (ECPA), 133–135,
Ellison-Potter, Patricia, 147
encryption, 42, 46–50
European Union (EU), 117, 123, 127, 131–132, 153–154, 156, 158–159, 167
eye contact, 150–151

F

facial recognition, 104–106, 108–109, 124, 134, 139, 166
First Amendment, 16, 53, 64–71, 73–74, 77, 83, 92, 165–166

G

gang databases, 115–119
Google, 15, 21, 82–83, 85, 111, 113, 130, 155–156, 159–161, 163
government, 15–16
  blocking internet access, 54
  Federal Communications Commission (FCC), 24–25, 27, 66

H

Harvey, Adam, 108

Index

I

IBM, 106, 108
India, 88, 153–156
internet, 14, 18
    age verification, 31, 59, 61–62
    anonymity, 15, 127, 141–146, 148–152, 163, 167
    broadband, 20–23, 25–27
    cookies, 120–123
    cyberbullying, 145, 149, 151, 170
    entertainment, 42, 86, 89–91
    friction, 121–123
    "kill switch," 54–56
    political, use of, 21–23, 54–55, 57, 78, 80, 86–90, 112
    purchases, 15, 41, 44, 121
    "right to be forgotten," (RTBF) 153, 159
    Web 2.0, 15
    Wi-Fi, 22
Internet Innovation Alliance, 24

K

Kaushik, Ashutosh, 153–156
Kazakhstan, 54–58, 165

L

Lobel, Orly, 95, 136–137, 163

M

Mann, Leon, 146–147
marginalized communities, 77, 79, 141, 167
    LGBTQIA+, 143
    people of color, 106, 118
mental health, 30–32
Microsoft, 37, 39, 68, 106, 108, 156
Milgram, Stanley, 122
misinformation, 15–16, 53, 56, 82–84, 138, 166,

N

Negroponte, Nicholas, 14

O

optimism, 14–15, 88, 140

P

parents, 19, 28–31, 60, 63, 147, 165
Patriot Act, 107
personal data, 15, 49, 111–112, 114, 131–132, 155, 166
phones, 22, 27, 61, 105, 107 121, 154
    iPhone, 105, 112,
police, 95–101, 103–104, 106, 115, 117–119, 124, 139, 142, 166
    data, use of, 98, 115–116
    predictive policing, 97–103
Postmes, Tom, 147–148
Public Knowledge, 75, 78–79, 81

R

Russia, 56, 89, 90, 92, 132

S

school, 13, 18, 31, 57

175 |

Section 230, 53, 75–85, 93, 166
  Communications Decency Act, 82–83
social media, 15–16, 28–33, 53, 64–66, 68–70, 72, 74–75, 77, 82–84, 87–88, 92, 95, 113, 117, 124, 127, 132, 142–144, 156, 162–163, 165–166
  Facebook, 15–16, 21, 30, 33, 65, 69–73, 76, 82–83, 85, 105, 108, 112–113, 124, 130–132
  Parler, 66
  TikTok, 29
  Twitter, 15, 33, 64–66, 68–70, 72, 76, 82–83, 121, 156
  YouTube, 29, 65, 76, 151, 159, 162
Supreme Court, 64–66, 69, 71–72, 74, 156
surveillance
  and inequality, 138
  by corporations, 95
  by government, 16, 58, 95
  by law enforcement, 104, 106, 108–109, 124, 133–134
  online, 55, 120–122, 136, 166
  "surveillance capitalism" 15

T

teachers, 28, 30–31
teenagers (teens), 18–19, 28, 32–33, 51, 147, 158, 162
Trump, Donald, 64–68, 84, 116
Turkey, 87–88

V

virtual private networks (VPNs), 57, 60, 62